EXTREME FAITH *for* EXTREME EVANGELISM

10-Week Bible Study for
Radically Sharing the Gospel
Through Signs, Wonders, and Miracles

PAUL WILLIAMS

HIGH BRIDGE BOOKS
HOUSTON

LIFE of FAITH in CHRIST MINISTRIES

Contents

Preface

IN THE GOSPEL OF JOHN, Jesus said, "Very truly I tell you, whoever believes in me will do the works I have been doing, and they will do even greater things than these, because I am going to the Father." (John 14:12). It is this verse that has fueled the journey my wife, Michelle, and I embarked upon in 2011. It is this verse that forms the foundation of this book.

Our early efforts at ministry began in 2000 when Michelle and I participated in our first church missionary trip to two prisons in Mazatlán, Mexico. The experience not only transformed our perspective on evangelism but also imbued us with increased courage to preach and teach the Word of God.

In 2001, we began a small group meeting in our home, a modest endeavor that continued for five years. It was a period of immense spiritual growth, as we ministered to different types of people, learning to adapt our approach to their unique personalities and individual spiritual needs. Later, we received formal training in Christian marriage counseling, which launched our marriage counseling ministry that continues today.

Our passion for studying and understanding God's Word led us to Bible College. It was a deeply transformative two-year experience that culminated in us both earning an Associate's Degree in Biblical Studies. I later completed an additional year of study, resulting in my formal ordination as a minister of the gospel of Jesus Christ.

My deep fervor for God's Word the Bible was originally ignited in me as a child thanks to my strict parents. I was born into a family deeply rooted in faith where the Word of God was revered and intensely studied. My homeschooling was centered around a deeply conservative Bible curriculum, which demanded regular memorization and recitation of entire chapters of Scripture verbatim without error. These early experiences laid the foundation of my lifelong commitment to daily Bible study and prayer, a commitment that continues to thrive today.

In December 2011, an astonishing event shook my very core - I was healed instantly of five chronic diseases while reading the Bible alone by myself in a hotel room during a business trip to San Antonio, Texas. My radical instantaneous healing served as the catalyst for my first book, *"Expect to Believe: 90 Bible Study Devotionals to Activate Your Faith for the Impossible."* This book encapsulates my journey of faith and the consequent many miraculous healings I have been blessed of God be a conduit for in many people's lives.

Over the years since my healing, we have had the privilege of touching thousands of lives and witnessing many hundreds of instantaneous on-the-spot, profound miraculous healings – the blind seeing, the lame walking, the deaf hearing, and the sick raised to new health and vitality, just as our Lord Jesus did Himself and said His disciples would do.

Today, wherever I travel, whether for business or ministry, the healing touch of Jesus has instantaneously raised up the sick – unbelievers, atheists, Muslims, Hindus -- in cabs, buses, airplanes, stores, shopping malls, business meetings, and by phone calls and video conference sessions to distant places and even amazingly enough once by cell phone text message!

As you delve into the pages of this book, it is my hope and prayer that you receive insight, understanding, practical guidance and inspiration from the many scriptures and testimonies in this book. I pray your faith in Jesus and in God's Word the Bible rises until you are performing the same miracles, signs, and wonders that Jesus performed during His time on earth as He said we would (John 14:12).

Welcome, dear reader, to a journey towards healing, transformation, and a deepened faith in our Lord Jesus Christ.

—**Paul Williams**
   Life of Faith in Christ Ministries
   Houston, Texas USA
   August 2023

Acknowledgements

THIS BOOK WOULD NOT BE possible without the earnest prayers and tireless contributions of the following individuals:

- Michelle Williams, my wife-for-life ministry partner in everything who is my biggest booster, backer, exhorter, and supporter in the world.

- Brian Desilets, my close friend, dear brother in Christ, and perpetually upbeat business partner who is a co-instructor of our ministry's Extreme Faith for Extreme Evangelism video class series which accompanies this book. Brian is deeply blessed with an amazing prophetic gift of healing. God has used to heal many hundreds of people in dramatic on-the-spot fashion on the streets and in stores and everywhere he goes.

- Sylvia Swan, senior editor of this book who cheerfully performed countless hours of work battling through a series of unexpected crises and limited time constraints.

I am deeply grateful as well to several devoted prayer warriors and gifted content contributors who through much prayer and seeking the leading of the Holy Spirit created the highly valuable *"WALKING IT OUT - Class Assignment"* exercises that appear at the end of each chapter in this book. These important contributors appear here in alphabetical order by last name:

- Patricia Lucas
- Stacy Smith
- Deborah Wallace

About This Book

THIS WORKBOOK CAN BE used as a standalone resource or as a study guide companion to our inspired instructor-led online _free_ video training offered through our ministry website at _lifeoffaithinchrist.org_.

Our no-charge online video training offers deeply insightful and valuable complementary to each lesson in this workbook. As an example, this book contains dozens of abbreviated outlines of our class instructors' many personal miraculous healing testimonies, while their full testimonies as shared personally by each can be found online. These testimonies are marked through the book by this icon.

To access our free online video training here, use your smartphone to scan the barcode below or use your web browser to visit _www.lifeoffaithinchrist.org._

Life of Faith in Christ Ministries
Houston, Texas USA
Website: lifeoffaithinchrist.org
Email: info@lifeoffaithinchrist.org

1

Daily Close Intimacy with God

HERE ARE OUR LEARNING OBJECTIVES for Lesson 1 of this 10-week Bible Study series:

- Grow to love the Person and Presence of Jesus more than ever before, so that He becomes intimately more real than ever before in our busy daily lives.

- Understand the incredible power of the words we speak.

- Learn to "read-pray" God's Word to make it come alive in our spirits and hearts.

- Grow our faith to *expect* to hear the Holy Spirit speak as we read-pray God's Word.

- Begin learning how to accurately distinguish between God's voice and our enemy's. (This is the first of two lessons on this subject.)

_____

_____

_____

_____

_____

1.1 Open Our Hearts to a New Move of God

Your class instructors understand how difficult it can be to open ourselves to new ideas and new ways of doing things. Nevertheless, try to be as open as you can to the possibility that God is ready to do something new in your life in a new way:

- Isaiah 43:19 NIV (God):

  See, I am doing a new thing! Now it springs up; **do you not perceive it?** I am making a way in the wilderness and streams in the wasteland.

- Mark 2:21-22 NIV (Jesus):

  21 No one sews a patch of unshrunk cloth on an old garment. Otherwise, the new piece will pull away from the old, making the tear worse. And no one pours new wine into old wineskins.

  22 Otherwise, the wine will burst the skins, and both the wine and the wineskins will be ruined. **No, they pour new wine into new wineskins.**

Beginning with this class today, we can individually choose to ask the Holy Spirit to open our minds and hearts to God's Word in ways we might have overlooked, misunderstood, or not fully understood or applied before now.

1.2 Class Kickoff: Instructor Testimonies

 <u>For the full video recorded testimony, see page 5.</u>

Class instructors Paul and Brian will begin this class series by giving their personal testimonies[1]. Both testimonies will start with the present-day miraculous events they are privileged to be a part of now. Then each will go back to their respective early childhood upbringings to discuss key triggers which God has used to build strong faith in Him and His Word, resulting in a significant move of God in their lives.

Their testimonies will vividly illustrate how an intense pursuit of and obedience to God's Word and the Holy Spirit builds extreme faith, which in turn directly results in extreme evangelism, physical healing, prophesy, and other dramatic manifestations of the Holy Spirit. This understanding will be used as an aspirational foundation to set up the learning material that follows over this 10-week class series.

---

[1] This workbook can be used as a standalone resource or used in combination with free online instructor-led training. For information, see "About this Book" preceding this chapter.

_____

_____

_____

Now that you have completed prayerfully watching both testimonies, here are three key lessons drawn from Paul's intense 21-day fast and his subsequent radical healings and blessings of the Holy Spirit:

- Key takeaway lesson 1: <u>God responds to our faith</u> when it is *spoken with our lips* and put into *action* (much more on both from the Bible are coming up in Lessons 2 and 3):
  - o Hebrews 11:6 NIV:
    And without faith it is impossible to please God, because anyone who comes to him **must believe that he exists** and that he **rewards those who earnestly seek him**.

- Key takeaway lesson 2: <u>God responds to our desire for Him</u> when we make Him more important than everything else and seek Him with all that we are and everything we have. It comes down to this: **just how much do we want the Living God?** Jacob literally risked everything he had pursuing his blessing, but he prevailed as shown in this scripture passage:
  - o Genesis 32:24-29 NIV:
    24 So Jacob was left alone, and a man wrestled with him till daybreak.
    25 When the man saw that he could not overpower him, **he touched the socket of Jacob's hip so that his hip was wrenched as** he wrestled with the man.
    26 Then the man said, "Let me go, for it is daybreak."
    But Jacob replied, **"I will not let you go unless you bless me."** [...]
    29 **...<u>Then</u> he blessed him there.**

- Key takeaway lesson 3: <u>God responds to sacrifice</u> (fasting and prayer):
  - o John 6:35, 57-58, 63 NIV (Jesus):
    35 Then Jesus declared, **"I am the bread of life.** Whoever comes to me will never go hungry, and whoever believes in me will never be

thirsty.
[...]
57 Just as the living Father sent me and I live because of the Father, so the one who feeds on me will live because of me.
58 **This is the bread that came down from heaven.** Your ancestors ate manna and died, **but whoever feeds on this bread will live forever.** [...]
63 The Spirit gives life; the flesh counts for nothing. **The words I have spoken to you—they are full of the Spirit and life."**

_____

_____

_____

_____

_____

1.3 Steps to Abiding in God's Power & Presence

Where should we start in our quest to walk in a deeper daily anointing of God's Presence, Holy Spirit power, and fulfilled promises from His Word?

The **first step** and most crucial step of all is **Salvation:** being individually born-again by asking God to forgive us of our sins and making Jesus Christ the Lord and Savior of our lives. **Salvation is the vital prerequisite to everything else in this book.**

Therefore, if you are not a born-again Christian, please pray this prayer from your heart and mean it:

> Jesus, thank you for suffering and dying for my sins. Thank you for taking my place so that I do not to go to hell, but instead can have everlasting life. Forgive me of my sins Jesus! I make you both Savior and Lord of my life. Transform me into your image and teach me how to think and act like you. Amen.

The **second step** is the infilling of the Holy Spirit within us, as evidenced by the gift of speaking in tongues. If you have not yet been filled with the Holy Spirit as evidenced by speaking in tongues, then beginning today over the next ten weeks you will have opportunities to seek the Holy Spirit in this manner. You may also alternatively or additionally seek the infilling of the Holy Spirit in a local church which actively believes in and teaches on this subject.

The **third step** is outlined over the remainder of this chapter.

_____

_____

_____

_____

_____

1.4 Who Is the Holy Spirit and What Does He Do?

This powerful 10-week class is primarily designed for born-again Christians who have already received the indwelling of the mighty Holy Spirit as evidenced by speaking in tongues or have been actively seeking the Holy Spirit in this manner.

Those in our class who may need a primer on the Holy Spirit to understand who He is, what does He do, and what is His purpose should refer to Appendix A, *"Introduction to the Holy Spirit"* for a scripture-packed overview.

_____

_____

_____

_____

_____

1.5 The Anointing, Power, and Presence of the Holy Spirit

For those who are saved and have the infilling of the Holy Spirit as evidenced by speaking in tongues, we commend you!

However, as part of our Step 3 in today's lesson we will challenge you to go still further by seeking:

- A return to your first love for Jesus (see Revelations 2:4).

- A deeper, thorough understanding of God's Word (scripture).

- To abide in a consistent daily deeper impartation of the anointing, power, and <u>presence</u> of the Holy Spirit than what you may have previously.

So, what is the *anointing* of the Holy Spirit? As an introduction to this topic, the *anointing* can be thought of as being His manifest (*tangible*) power, presence, leading and gifting, which when combined with the skillful application of God's Word gives us a powerful offensive weapon against our enemy:

- Ephesians 6:7 NIV (the Armor of God):
  Take the helmet of salvation and **the sword of the Spirit, which is the word of God.**

Here are several scriptures about the tangible (perceptible) anointing, power, and presence of the Holy Spirit:

- Luke 4:17-19 NIV:
  17 and the scroll of the prophet Isaiah was handed to (Jesus). Unrolling it, he found the place where it is written:
  18 **'The Spirit of the Lord is on me**, because **he has anointed m**e to proclaim good news to the poor. **He has sent me** to proclaim freedom for the prisoners and **recovery of sight for the blind, to set the oppressed free,**
  19 to proclaim the year of the Lord's favor.'

- Ezekiel 1:3 NLT: The Lord gave this message to Ezekiel son of Buzi, a priest, beside the Kebar River in the land of the Babylonians, and he **felt the hand of the Lord take hold of him.**

- Jeremiah 15:16-17 NLT:
  16 When I discovered your words, I devoured them. They are my joy and my heart's delight, for I bear your name, O Lord God of Heaven's Armies.
  17 I never joined the people in their merry feasts. I sat alone because **your hand was on me**. I was filled with indignation at their sins.

- Luke 1:26, 35 NIV:
  In the sixth month of Elizabeth's pregnancy, God sent the angel Gabriel to Nazareth, a town in Galilee,
  [..]

The angel answered (Mary), 'The Holy Spirit **will come on you**, and the power of the Most High **will overshadow you**. So the holy one to be born will be called the Son of God.

- Matthew 3:16-17 and 4:1 NIV:
  3:16 As soon as Jesus was baptized, he went up out of the water. At that moment heaven was opened, and he saw the Spirit of God descending like a dove **and alighting on him**.
  3:17 And a voice from heaven said, 'This is my Son, whom I love; with him I am well pleased.'
  4:1 Then Jesus **was led** by the Spirit into the wilderness to be tempted by the devil.

- Acts 10:38 NIV: …God **anointed** Jesus of Nazareth **with the Holy Spirit and with power**. Then Jesus went around doing good and healing all who were oppressed by the devil, for God **was with him**.

- Acts 6:5, 8, 10 NIV:
  5 This proposal pleased the whole group. **They chose Stephen, a man full of faith and of the Holy Spirit**; also, Philip, Procorus, Nicanor, Timon, Parmenas, and Nicolas from Antioch, a convert to Judaism.
  [...]
  8 **Now Stephen, a man full of God's grace and power, performed great wonders and signs among the people.**
  [...]
  10 But they could not stand up against the **wisdom the Spirit gave him** as he spoke.

Our personal goal should be to become so filled with the Holy Spirit and remain in this state so that He overflows out from within us all of the time, as Jesus teaches here:

- John 7:37-39 NIV:
  37 On the last and greatest day of the festival, Jesus stood and said in a loud voice, 'Let anyone who is thirsty come to me and drink.
  38 Whoever believes in me, as Scripture has said, **rivers of living water will flow from within them**.'
  39 By this he meant **the Spirit**, whom those who believed in him were later to receive. Up to that time the Spirit had not been given, since Jesus had not yet been glorified.

If we continue our pursuit of God in this manner, over time the anointing of the Holy Spirit can build so powerfully and overflow (radiate) so strongly on and from us, that others in our presence (the unsaved in particular) may experience pronounced physical effects throughout an entire room you enter. Your entrance can cause normal-appearing but nevertheless demon-oppressed or demon-possessed people to immediately turn and glare with undisguised hostility to your presence as you silently enter a room or even a church (gasp!) from behind.

At its extreme, the anointing of the Holy Spirit can involuntarily and instantly level an entire roomful of people at once, including even hardened unsaved sinners, who are neither seeking God nor wanting Him in their lives. Later in this 10-week class you will hear an incredible testimony of how 200 law enforcement officers attending a secular training class were suddenly leveled to the floor in weeping public confession of sin and seeking repentance and salvation by a sudden, unexpected manifestation of the power of Holy Spirit. This event was triggered a single Spirit-filled believer in the room whom God used as a catalyst, all *without* preaching and *without* an altar call!

 The important part to remember and our key takeaway point here is this: the stronger the anointing of the Holy Spirit becomes upon us, the more often and pronounced the manifestations of God's glory become for all to see in this earthly natural realm in the form of signs, wonders, and miracles. Let us all recommit tonight to earnestly seek the Holy Ghost in His fullness in our lives.

Coming up next: *how* to seek and *keep* the powerful anointing of the Holy Spirit all throughout the busy work week, not just in church or in special events.

_____

_____

_____

_____

_____

1.6 Seeking the Anointing of the Holy Spirit

In order to daily *abide* (remain) in the overflowing of the anointing of Holy Spirit as just described, we must begin by loving and seeking our God with **all** our whole heart, mind, and soul. And not only this, but **we should *continue* to seek Him until we find Him.** In both the Old and New Testaments of the Bible we see examples of how those who are seeking God and His blessings must forsake the all-too-comfortable draw of "good enough" complacency to pursue God with all their hearts until He is found in His fullness:

- Revelation 2:4, 3:15-19 NIV (Jesus):
  4 Yet I hold this against you: **You have forsaken the love you had at first.**
  5 Consider how far you have fallen! **Repent and do the things you did at first.** If you do not repent, I will come to you and remove your lampstand from its place.

- Revelation 3:15-19 NIV (Jesus):
  15 **I know your deeds, that you are neither cold nor hot.** I wish you were either one or the other!
  16 So, because you are lukewarm—neither hot nor cold—I am about to spit you out of my mouth.
      [...]
  19 Those whom I love I rebuke and discipline. **So be earnest and repent.**

- Romans 12:9, 11 NIV:
  9 Love must be sincere. **Hate what is evil**; cling to what is good.
      [...]
  11 Never be lacking in zeal, **but keep your spiritual fervor**, serving the Lord.

- Deuteronomy 4:29 NIV: But if from there you seek the Lord your God, you will find him if you seek him with **all** your heart and with **all** your soul.

- Jerimiah 29:13 NIV: You will seek me and find me **when** you seek me with **all** your heart.

- Matthew 22:37 NIV: Jesus replied, 'Love the Lord your God with **all** your heart and with **all** your soul and with **all** your mind.'

- John 14:21 NIV: Whoever has my commands and keeps them is the one who loves me. The one who loves me will be loved by my Father, **and I too will love them and show myself to them.**

One of the first manifestations of Jesus and the Holy Spirit dwelling within us is the softening of our hearts with genuine love for others:

- Galatians 5:22, 23 NIV:
  22 But the fruit of the Spirit is **love**, joy, peace, forbearance, kindness, goodness, faithfulness,
  23 gentleness and self-control. Against such things there is no law.

- 1 Corinthians 14:1 NIV: **Follow the way of love** and eagerly desire gifts of the Spirit, **especially prophecy**.

- 1 John 4:16 NIV: And so, we know and rely on the love God has for us. **God is love.** Whoever lives in love lives in God, and God in them.

God Himself *is* love, and He births His love within us through the Holy Spirit's fruit of love. To be effective, Biblical prophecy must flow from the first fruit of the Holy Spirit in our lives, which is love:

- 1 Corinthians 13:1 "If I speak in the tongues of men or of angels, but do not have love, I am only a resounding gong or a clanging cymbal."

The deeper and stronger the anointing of the Holy Spirit becomes within us, the greater our love for God and others become and the more the gifts of the Holy Spirit -- including prophesy and the gifts of healing (plural)-- manifest within us.

For this reason, throughout this 10-week class series we will heavily focus on how to **continuously seek and dwell in the anointing of the Holy Spirit** around the clock and throughout the work week everywhere we go, and not just in church on Sunday or during an occasional church mission trip.

_____

_____

_____

_____

_____

_____

_____

_____

1.7 The Power of Our Words

As we continue seeking God earnestly with all our heart, soul and mind beginning today for the next 10 weeks, at the same time we have a second pressing priority in our quest for God in His fullness in our lives. Here it is: we must learn how not to defeat ourselves faster than the Holy Spirit can birth His fruits, gifts, and His tangible anointing of God's mighty power within us.

This is because it is **far easier** than even most experienced charismatic Christians realize **to curse ourselves and bring about our own defeat** by our enemy… especially when it comes to physical healing and the casting out of demons. This includes both our ability to easily receive our own healing and stay healed, as well as our prayers for the healing of others.

Over this 10-week class we will learn much more about this subject, but as a start for now here are some foundational scriptures on speaking *life* rather than *death* over ourselves, our families, careers, and our problems!

- Proverbs 18:21 NIV: "**The tongue has the power of life and death**, and those who love it will eat its fruit. "

- Romans 10:9-10 NIV: "If you declare **with your mouth,** "Jesus is Lord," and believe in your heart that God raised him from the dead, you will be saved. For it is with your heart that you believe and are justified, and it is **with your mouth** that you profess your faith and are saved."

- 2 Corinthians 4:13 NIV: "It is written: 'I believed; therefore, I have **spoken**.' Since we have that same spirit of faith, we also believe and therefore **speak**."

- Ephesians 4:29 NIV: "Do not let any unwholesome talk come out of your **mouths**, but only what is **helpful** for building others up according to their needs, that it may **benefit** those who listen."

- Matthew 12:36-37 NLT (Jesus): And I tell you this, you must give an account on judgment day for every idle word you speak. The words you say will either acquit you or condemn you."

Here is an uncomplicated way to remember the Biblical concept being presented:

"What we say about the problems we are going through will result in us either blessing or cursing ourselves. It is our choice."[2]

As a vivid illustration of this from God's Word, let us consider an important question: When did David win his victory over Goliath? Was it:

1) When David physically fought the giant, or

2) Was it spiritually before David even stepped on the battlefield to fight the giant?

For the answer, let us read God's Word and find out:

- 1 Samuel 17:45-47 NIV:
  45 David said to the Philistine, "You come against me with sword and spear and javelin, but I come against you in the name of the Lord Almighty, the God of the armies of Israel, whom you have defied.
  46 **This day the Lord will deliver you into my hands, and I'll strike you down and cut off your head. This very day** I will give the carcasses of the Philistine army to the birds and the wild animals, and the whole world will know that there is a God in Israel.
  47 All those gathered here will know that it is not by sword or spear that the Lord saves; for the battle is the Lord's, **and He will give all of you into our hands.**"

Dear friends, David won his victory before the fight even started by his bold proclamation of faith out loud for all to hear. Notice how David was *specific* in proclaiming *exactly* what he expected God to do for him. David publicly proclaimed that God would give him total victory that same day -- not only the death of the giant, but of all the giant's army of solder friends, too. What David spoke was exactly what he received from God.

This New Testament scripture backs this concept up:

- 2 Corinthians 4:13 NIV
  It is written: 'I believed; **therefore, I have spoken**.' Since we have that same spirit of faith, we also believe and **therefore speak**.

---

[2] Excerpted from Lesson 83 from the book *Expect to Believe: 90 Bible Devotionals to Increase Your Faith For the Impossible* by Paul Williams of Life of Faith in Christ Ministries.

So, here is a question for each of us individually: do *you* pray boldly in faith like this? Do *you* declare your faith aloud with your lips for all your family, friends, and more to hear?

If you are accustomed to praying weak, "God-bless-me" type prayers that can mean anything or nothing, **then start toda**y learning to pray specifically and boldly to proclaim your faith aloud with your lips.

From one end of the Bible to the other, God's Word is clear that He is pleased by His servants' faith. The bolder our faith is, the bigger His miracles are on our behalf.[3]

_____

_____

_____

_____

_____

_____

_____

_____

_____

_____

1.8 God's Word + The Holy Spirit = Great Power

Let us discuss what happens when "the sword of the Spirit, which is the Word of God" (Ephesians 6:17) is spoken out loud by our lips in the name of Jesus through the power and leading of Holy Spirit (read this again!).

Notice what Jesus our example did when He was led into the wilderness by the Holy Spirit to be tempted by Satan (Matthew 4:1). Jesus did not use His own words, but rather quoted scripture to Satan in order to defeat him.

_____

[3] Excerpted from Chapter 5, *Expect to Believe: 90 Bible Devotionals to Increase Your Faith For the Impossible.*

EXTREME FAITH for EXTREME EVANGELISM

In the battle of scripture that followed in Mathew chapter 4, both Jesus and Satan understood that God's Word was the ultimate arbitrator. Jesus out-quoted Satan and won the confrontation. Let us read this for ourselves:

- Matthew 4:4, 7, 10, 11 NIV:
  4 Jesus answered (the devil), '**It is written**: 'Man shall not live on bread alone, but on every word that comes from the mouth of God' (reference to Deuteronomy 8:3)
  6 (The devil) said, 'throw yourself down. For **it is written**…'
  (reference to Psalm 91:11,12).
  7 Jesus answered him, '**It is also written**: Do not put the Lord your God to the test' (reference to Deuteronomy 6:16).
  10 Jesus said to him, 'Away from me, Satan! For **it is written**: Worship the Lord your God and serve him only' (reference to Deuteronomy 6:13).
  11 Then the devil left him, and angels came and attended him.

Notice how Jesus did not quote what his earthly father Joseph or his mother Mary had taught him, or his Rabbi, a Priest, a Bishop, or a Pastor, or what someone on TV said (!). Instead, acting as our example in all things, Jesus quoted God's Word to Satan…. and likewise, so should we.

Also, just as importantly, notice how Jesus living as a man on this earth knew exactly which scripture to quote to Satan in response to each of our enemy's attacks. Jesus did not repeat the same two or three "go-to" scriptures each time, such as today's widely used catch-all scripture "no weapon formed against me will prosper" excerpted from Isaiah 54:17, etc.

Obviously, Jesus growing up as a human being just like us, had invested His time wisely over the years in learning God's Word well. So should we.

Jesus promises us a significant payoff in our everyday lives if we will take the time to commit God's Word to memory as He did:

- John 15:7 NIV: (Jesus): "If you remain in me and **my words <u>remain</u> in you**, ask whatever you wish, and it will be done for you."

_____

_____

_____

1.9 Making God Much More Real in Our Daily Lives

Class challenge: read Psalms chapter 139 in its entirety tonight in your Bibles. For the time being, we will read selected passages from this chapter now:

Psalm chapter 139 NLT:
For the choir director: A psalm of David.
1 O Lord, you have examined my heart
  and **know everything about me.**
2 You know when I sit down or stand up.
  You know my thoughts even when I'm far away.
3 You see me when I travel
  and when I rest at home.
  You know everything I do.
4 You **know what I am going to say**
  even before I say it, Lord.
5 **You go before me and follow me**.
  You place your hand of blessing on my head.
6 Such knowledge is too wonderful for me,
  too great for me to understand!
7 **I can never escape from your Spirit!**
  I can never get away from your presence!
8 If I go up to heaven, **you are there;**
  if I go down to the grave (Sheol), **you are there**.
9 If I ride the wings of the morning,
  if I dwell by the farthest oceans,
10 **even there** your hand will guide me,
  and your strength will support me.
11 I could ask the darkness to hide me
  and the light around me to become night—
12 **but even in darkness I cannot hide from you.**
To you the night shines as bright as day.
  Darkness and light are the same to you.

13 You made all the delicate, inner parts of my body
   and knit me together in my mother's womb.
14 Thank you for making me so wonderfully complex!
   Your workmanship is marvelous—how well I know it.
15 **You watched me as I was being formed in utter seclusion,** as I was woven
   together in the dark of the womb.
16 **You saw me before I was born.**
   Every day of my life was recorded in your book.
Every moment was laid out
   before a single day had passed.
17 How precious are your thoughts about me, O God.
   They cannot be numbered!
18 I can't even count them;
   they outnumber the grains of sand!
And when I wake up,
   you are still with me!
   [… skip to verse 23…]
23 Search me, O God, and know my heart.
   test me and know my anxious thoughts.
24 **Point out anything in me that offends you,
   and lead me along the path of everlasting life.**

To further emphasize the reality of the supernatural realm –both good and bad—that constantly surrounds us wherever we go, here is an important New Testament scripture passage that backs this up. In reference to all the Old Testament hero of faith who have passed on before us in Hebrews chapter 11, the apostle Paul goes on to write:

- Hebrews 12:1-4 NIV:
  1 Therefore, since we are surrounded by such a **huge crowd of witnesses** to the life of faith, let us strip off every weight that slows us down, especially the sin that so easily trips us up. And let us run with endurance the race God has set before us.
  2 We do this by **keeping our eyes on Jesus**, the champion who initiates and perfects our faith. Because of the joy awaiting him, he endured the cross, disregarding its shame. Now he is seated in the place of honor beside God's throne.

3 Think of all the hostility he endured from sinful people; then you won't become weary and give up.

4 After all, you have not yet given your lives in your struggle against sin.

1.10 Illustrative Testimonies

For the full video recorded testimony, see page 5.

Testimony 1: God revealed class instructor Paul's innermost thoughts through a friend, a prophet. Paul felt like a "fish in a bowl" for three months afterward.

Testimony 2: The Holy Spirit giving Paul a vision of his friend and his wife and parents in a dark den watching TV. The "tour" went through the walls and the refrigerator. Oddly, the interior of the refrigerator although lacking light nevertheless was not dark, but rather was evenly lit (as just read in Ps. 139:12). Paul was able to see and hear their five-way disagreement and even clearly hear the unspoken thoughts of each person in the order they thought it. The vision was later confirmed in every detail by his friend.

EXTREME FAITH for EXTREME EVANGELISM

1.11 God's Word Will Change Us

Let us understand the power of God's Word:

- Hebrews 4:12 NLT: For the Word of God is alive and powerful. It is sharper than the sharpest two-edged sword, cutting between soul and spirit, between joint and marrow. It exposes our innermost thoughts and desires.

- John 6:63 NLT (Jesus): The Spirit alone gives eternal life. Human effort accomplishes nothing. **And the very words I have spoken to you are spirit and life.**

- John 15:7 NLT: "**But if you remain in me and my words remain in you**, you may ask for anything you want, and it will be granted!"

- 2 Timothy 3:15-17 NLT:
  15 ...and how from infancy you have known the Holy Scriptures, **which are able to make you wise for salvation through faith in Christ Jesus.**
  16 All Scripture is inspired by God and is **useful to teach us what is true and to make us realize what is wrong** in our lives. It **corrects us** when we are wrong and **teaches us** to do what is right.
  17 God uses it to **prepare and equip his peo**ple to do every good work.

From these scriptures we learn that the Word of God is alive and active and as a result it corrects and teaches us. Here are more scriptures which shed light on the impact God's Word *will* have on us if we let it: .

- John 10:4-5 NIV (Jesus): When he has brought out all his own, he goes on ahead of them, and his sheep follow him **because they know his voice.**
  5 But they will never follow a stranger; in fact, they will run away from him because they do not recognize a stranger's voice.

- James 1:21 NLT: So get rid of all the filth and evil in your lives, and humbly accept the word God has planted in your hearts, **for it has the power to save your souls.**

1.12 Seven Steps to an Intimate Relationship with God

Let us put what we learned today into action, since we know that "faith without deeds is useless" according to James 2:20 NIV. We can do this by allowing the Holy Spirit to begin the process of changing us as we "read-pray" God's Word the scriptures. **Adding a Biblically based food-fast is even better and when combined with increased study of God's Word and prayer can lead to a significant breakthrough.**

A key goal of this week's class is to begin building a much closer, much more intimate relationship with God. Thankfully, God's Word shows us exactly how to do so in 7 steps in James 4:7-10 NIV (quoted following).

So as a class exercise[4] we will closely examine these 7 steps, one concept and one sentence at a time (follow along in your Bibles):

James 4:7-10 NIV:

Step 1: "Submit yourselves, then, to God." (Verse 7)
Action item: Lord, I want every part of my heart, mind, and soul to be subject to Your Will for me. Instruct me, and I commit in advance to do whatever You tell me to do.

Step 2: "Resist the devil, and he will flee from you." (Verse 7)
Action item: Jesus, I take authority in Your Name over myself, my thoughts, and my actions. Satan, I rebuke you and the power of your temptations over me in the name of Jesus. You have no power over me.

Step 3: "Come near to God and He will come near to you." (Verse 8)
Action item: O God, as told in the Parable of the Prodigal Son, I know You will run to meet me more than halfway (Luke 15:20). However, the first part of my journey toward You is my decision and my responsibility. I, therefore, commit to pursuing You, God, until I find You (Jerimiah 29:13).

Step 4: "Wash your hands, you sinners, and purify your hearts, you double-minded." (Verse 8)
Action item: Lord, I repent of my sins, and I turn away from them. Holy Spirit, examine every part of me and show me where I am wrong and where I need to change. As You do so, I will change my behavior and not delay or make excuses. I am committed to this process, and I will not slip back from it as I have on other occasions.

Step 5: "Grieve, mourn and wail." (Verse 9)

---

[4] This exercise is excerpted from Chapter 3, "Seven Steps to an Intimate Relationship with God" from the book *Expect to Believe: 90 Bible Devotionals to Increase Your Faith for the Impossible.*

Action item: I mourn the waste of time I have put myself and You through O God. I mourn for not being completely serious about my pursuit of You much sooner. I need You more than my daily food, so much so that I have lost much of my interest in food and am fasting to seek Your Heart and Your Will for me and my life.

Step 6: "Change your laughter to mourning and your joy to gloom." (Verse 9)
Action item: I realize the pursuit of You is serious business and requires my full attention. I am fasting to seek Your Face. Therefore, I set aside television, sports, games, and any foolishness so that nothing will distract me from what Your Word and Your Spirit are telling me.

Step 7: "Humble yourselves before the Lord, and He will lift you up." (Verse 10)
Action item: Everything that I am and everything that I have and will be Yours, O God. I am nothing without You. I pursue You expectantly and hungrily. I claim Your Promise that those who seek You diligently will find You (Jerimiah 29:13).

So… you may be wondering, does this seven-step process spelled out in James 4:7-10 really work? Of course, it does; no surprise there. The Word of God always works when we study it correctly and do our part in faith. God cannot be pleased without our faith (Hebrews 11:6), so we must have faith and expectantly claim God's favor and blessing upon us as we earnestly seek Him.

_____

_____

_____

_____

_____

_____

_____

_____

1.13 Over the Coming Weeks

What has been covered in this first lesson is the foundation of this *Extreme Faith for Extreme Evangelism* class. Therefore, begin the homework task of our action plan in in the next section.

During your daily "morning and evening sacrifice" (translation: investing in the meditative study of God's Word and communion with God in prayer), as you read-pray the scriptures begin listening in faith to hear the still small voice of the Holy Spirit speaking to you. This may begin as faint impressions on selected scripture passages or as references to other scriptures and will grow from there.

If you are finding it a challenge to truly love some of the people in your life, a daily assignment has been included in our action plan at the end of this chapter. Begin by asking the Holy Spirit to soften your heart and fill you with God's amazing love for all of His erring and sinful created beings. To grow in love is the heart of a true disciple of Jesus.

When we keep our sustained focus on the overwhelming love that God has for us, it becomes easier and in time easy to overflow with His amazing love toward others. This is important because God's miraculous power flowing through us is markedly more effective when our primary driving motivation is God's amazing love.

See you next week!

Additional Class Notes (Lesson One)

Your Personal Notes, Observations, and Class Activities

_____

_____

_____

_____

_____

_____

_____

_____

_____

_____

_____

_____

_____

_____

_____

_____

_____

_____

_____

_____

Questions for the Instructors or the class:

1. _____

_____

_____

_____

_____

2. _____

_____

_____

_____

_____

3. _____

_____

_____

_____

_____

1.14 Walking It Out – Class Assignment (LESSON ONE)

WALKING IT OUT Class Assignment *(LESSON ONE)*

OUR ACTION PLAN

Seek **JESUS** at a *level and depth that you may not have previously to* continually further develop and deepen your intimate, personal relationship with Jesus.

Read Daily: "Expect to Believe: 90 Bible Devotionals to Increase Your Faith for the Impossible" by Paul Williams (expect a close encounter with the Holy Spirit to happen while reading these devotionals daily).

Watch / Listen to the Class Lesson Videos; pause when needed to read-pray scriptures, work Action Plan steps, work Homework Challenges and Go Deeper **as** you go through your class notes AGAIN. *(Journaling revelations Holy Spirit has shown you)*

Review Weekly: Key Learning Objectives *(check off each one as you achieve the objectives of this week's lesson (see this chapter's Introduction). Ask the Holy Spirit to plant these objectives deep in your heart and mind and help put them into practice in your daily life.*

Suggested Action: fast, creating an intimate relationship with God: *(per section 1.2 apply the three key takeaways that the author learned).* God responds to fasting and prayer. ***Adding a Biblically based food-fast is even better and can aid in combination with God's Word and prayer to a significant breakthrough*** *(see section 1.12)* ***Speak aloud*** the action items in the seven steps taken from **James 4:7-10** *(especially steps 5& 6 (see section 1.12)).*

Daily abide in the overflow of the anointing of Holy Spirit *(as described in sections 1.5 and 1.6).* Ask the Holy Spirit **every day** to **soften your heart and fill you with God's amazing love** for Your fellow created human beings. Re-commit to earnestly seeking the Holy Ghost in His fullness in your life.

Daily read and apply the books of _John, Acts, and Ephesians_[5] *(see section 1.12)* using the "read-pray the Word approach" and the "Seven Steps to Intimate Relationship with God."

Set your God times: Ask God… How, When, Where, What?

For a primer or refresher about the Holy Spirit, read-pray the scripture-packed overview in **Appendix A**, "Introduction to the Holy Spirit" *(journal what is revealed by the Holy Spirit).*

Important: be careful to distinguish between God's voice and Satan's voice by **always** comparing every part you hear against scripture *(this is covered in considerable depth later in this book – as well as what can and often does easily happen if we do not).*

Make sure **your motives are solely based on love** specifically, God's love: *(read-pray and journal)*

- **1 Peter 4:8** NLT: Most important of all, continue to show deep love for each other, for love covers a multitude of sins.

- **1 Corinthians 16:14** NLT: And do everything with love.

- **2 John 1:6b**: Love means doing what God has commanded us, and He has commanded us **to love one another**, just as you heard from the beginning.

- **1 Corinthians 13:4-8** NLT: 4 Love is patient and kind. Love is not jealous or boastful or proud.
  5 or rude. It does not demand its own way. It is not irritable, and it keeps no record of being wronged.
  6 It does not rejoice about injustice but rejoices whenever the truth wins out.
  7 Love never gives up, never loses faith, is always hopeful, and endures through every circumstance.
  8 Prophecy and speaking in unknown languages and special knowledge will become useless. But love will last forever!

---

[5] In our observation, no other combination of three books in the Bible gives as much spiritual return for the time invested. These three books serve as an effective jumping point to real-pray the remainder of the entire Bible.

- **1 John 4:16:** We know how much God loves us, and we have put our trust in his love. **God is love**, and **all who live in love live in God**, and God lives in them.

Power of Our Words: Speak foundational scriptures on *life* rather than *death* over you, your family, careers, and your problems. Read, pray, reflect, and repent. *(see section 1.7)*

Start today to begin **learning to pray specifically and boldly to proclaim your faith aloud** with your lips.. *(see section 1.7)*

Read and reflect: Psalms chapter 139 in its entirety.

HOMEWORK CHALLENGE

1.What are the two goals of Life of Faith in Christ Ministries?

_____

_____

_____

_____

_____

_____

2. As per Paul's testimony: Why did work based religion not work?

_____

_____

_____

_____

2b. How does Paul Williams' story parallel to Apostle Paul in the Bible?

_____

_____

_____

_____

_____

_____

3. Why do we need the Holy Spirit in abundance?

_____

_____

How / When does this happen in a person's life?

_____

_____

_____

_____

4. How do you seek and keep the _powerful anointing_ of the Holy Spirit throughout the busy work week?

_____

_____

_____

_____

_____

5. One of the very first manifestations of Jesus and the Holy Spirit dwelling within us is the _____ for others.

6. How will you answer, "What good is speaking in tongues?"

_____

_____

7. Paul and Brian have learned to dwell in the anointing of the Holy Spirit _____.

How will / have you accomplish this?

_____

_____

_____

8. We can individually choose to ask the Holy Spirit to open our minds and hearts to _____ _____ in ways we might have overlooked, misunderstood, or not fully understood or applied before now.

9. To start our quest to walk in a deeper anointing of God's presence, Holy Spirit power and fulfilled promises from His Word, the first step is _____, the vital prerequisite to everything else in this class.

10. What are the seven steps to an intimate relationship with God? Where are they found in the Bible?

_____

_____

_____

_____

_____

_____

_____

_____

11. When did David win his battle over Goliath?

_____

_____

_____

_____

12. What must you change in order to not defeat yourself faster than the Holy Spirit can birth His *fruit, gifts,* and His *tangible anointing* of God's mighty power within you?

_____

_____

_____

_____

_____

13. List the ways the Word of God is alive and active and able to instruct and teach us:

_____

_____

_____

_____

_____

_____

_____

_____

GOING DEEPER (Journal Time)

1. Which attributes of the primary Bible study goal are you learning and/or operating in?

1b. Which attributes above do you need to learn more about to be ready in season?

_____

_____

2. What are your heartfelt beliefs regarding the scripture John 14:12? 2b. How are you allowing John 14:12 to work in your life?

_____

_____

3. To build a much closer, more intimate relationship with God, ask the Holy Spirit to give you a plan of action using the seven steps in James 4:7-10. Example: Lord, do I have little faith? What is my stopping block(s)? Lord, am I loving people? Why am I not loving people?

4. How did their testimonies vividly illustrate an intense pursuit of an obedience to God's Word? How did the Holy Spirit build Paul and Brian's extreme faith?

_____

_____

_____

_____

5. What would you do differently if you *knew* Jesus was coming back tomorrow? (see Mathew 25:13)

_____

_____

6. Throughout your day, start asking the Holy Spirit to lead and guide you in everything you do and say. You may want to journal what you are learning from the Holy Spirit.

2

Doing the Miracles That Jesus Did

2.1 Learning Objectives for Lesson 2

HERE ARE OUR LEARNING OBJECTIVES for our second class:

- Understand the healing commission that Jesus gave us.

- Learn how to physically heal the sick and injured on the spot like Jesus did.

- Begin understanding the importance of demonstrating our faith with **action** and how to do so (*there will be much more important learning material on this topic throughout this book*).

Let us get started.

2.2 Jesus Told His Disciples to Heal the Sick

It can require time to understand and embrace the reality that Jesus explicitly *expects* us as His disciples to follow His example by healing the sick and raising the dead. Thankfully, from a study of scripture we can see that Jesus has indeed equipped us with the mandate, knowledge, and authority we need to do so:

- John 14:12 NLT (Jesus):
  I tell you the truth, **anyone** who believes in me <u>**will**</u> **do the same works I have done,** and even greater works, because I am going to be with the Father.

- Matthew 10:1 NIV:
  Jesus called his twelve disciples to him and gave them authority to drive out impure spirits and to heal every disease and sickness.

- Mark: 16:17 NIV (Jesus):

EXTREME FAITH *for* EXTREME EVANGELISM

These miraculous signs **will** accompany those who believe: They **will** cast out demons in my name, and they **will** speak in new languages.
18 They **will** be able to handle snakes with safety, and if they drink anything poisonous, it won't hurt them. **They will be able to place their hands on the sick, and they will be healed.**

(Practical examples: "God Saves a Nation: The Story of Zambia, Africa" in Chapter 3)

2.3 How To Do the Works That Jesus Did

For us to do the works that Jesus did as our example, each of us individually must first know (absorb, understand, and live) three important foundational truths from God's Word. Here are three foundational truths that we must know as living truth in our spirits:

- **Who** am I in Christ?
- **What** authority do I have?
- **How** do I use my authority in Christ?

If we know these three things, a miracle will always occur[6].

---

*"When we know **who** we are in Christ, **what** authority we have, and **how** to use our authority, a miracle will occur every time. But if our enemy can disrupt our understanding of any one of these three things, then no miracle will occur."*
—*Brian Desilets, Class Instructor*

---

[6] "Disclaimer": This is assuming that the prerequisite conditions of faith, speaking God's Words with our lips and several other conditions are in place – all of which are explained in detail over the course of this 10-week class.

Let us carefully study these three critically important foundational truths in God's Word so we can absorb these truths deep into our spirits, minds, and hearts and be able to speak them forth and use them.

2.3.1 Foundational Truth #1 of 3: Who Am I in Christ?

Individual prayer: Holy Spirit, open my mind and heart to these truths in God's Word:

- 1 Peter 2:9 NLT:
  But you are not like that, for you are a **chosen people**. You are **royal priests**, a holy nation, God's **very own possession**. As a result, you can show others the goodness of God, for He called you out of the darkness into His wonderful light.

- Romans 8:17 NIV: Now if we are children, then we are heirs—heirs of God **and co-heirs with Christ**, if indeed we share in his sufferings in order that we may also share in his glory.

- John 17:22-23 NLT (Jesus' prayer to the Father):
  22 I have given them the glory you gave me, so they may be one as we are one.
  23 I am in them and you are in me. May they experience such perfect unity that the world will know that you sent me and **that you love them as much as you love me.**

- Hebrews 4:16 NLT:
  So let us come **boldly** to the throne of our gracious God. There we will receive his mercy, and we will find grace to help us when we need it most.

- Ephesians 3:12 NIV:
  In him (Christ) and through faith in him we may approach God **with freedom and confidence.**

Summary: We are the Father's own possession, "joint heirs" with Jesus Christ, royal priests unto our God, who the Father loves the same as He loves Jesus. (Jesus' blood won **total** victory for us... just wow - gasp!)
Let us allow this truth to settle deep down inside of us. As this reality grows in your spirit, mind, and heart, your prayers for others and yourself will dramatically increase in both boldness and persistence. Hallelujah!

_____

_____

_____

2.3.3 Foundational Truth #2 of 3: What Authority Do I Have?

Now that we fully know who we are in Christ, it is time to learn from God's Word the details of the authority we have been given.

Let us start by understanding the authority that our example Jesus had:

- Philippians 2:5-8 NLT:
  5 **You must have the same attitude that Christ Jesus had.**
  6 Though he was God, he did not think of equality with God as something to cling to.
  7 Instead, **he gave up his divine privileges;**
  he took the humble position of a **slave** (<< NIV: *"he made himself **nothing** by taking the **very nature of a servant**"*)
  and was born **as a human being.**
  When he appeared in human form,
  8 he humbled himself in obedience to God
  and died a criminal's death on a cross.

In the following scripture passage, we further see how Jesus did not heal by His own power, but rather Jesus healed by the anointing and power of the Holy Spirit upon Him… which we can optionally have also as we individually so choose:

- Isaiah 11:1-3 NIV (prophecy about Jesus, the coming Messiah):
  1 A shoot will come up from the stump of Jesse; from his roots a Branch will bear fruit.
  2 **The Spirit of the Lord will rest on him**— the Spirit of wisdom and of understanding, the Spirit of counsel and of might, the Spirit of the knowledge and fear of the Lord—
  3 and he will delight in the fear of the Lord. He will not judge by what he sees with his eyes, or decide by what he hears with his ears;

- Acts 10:38 NLT:

  …God **anointed** Jesus of Nazareth **with the Holy Spirit and with power.** <u>Then</u> Jesus went around doing good and healing all who were oppressed by the devil, **for God was with him.**

- John 3:34 NLT (John the Baptist):

  For he (Jesus) is sent by God. He speaks God's words, for God **gives him the Spirit without limit.**

In the following extremely important scripture passages from Ephesians chapters 1 and 2, we learn the *root source* of our authority is in heaven where **we are positioned spiritually at the right hand of the Father <u>*with*</u> our Lord and Savior Jesus Christ Himself:**

- Ephesians 1:18-23 NIV:

  18 "I pray that the **eyes of your heart may be enlightened** in order that you may **know** the hope to which He has called you, the riches of His glorious inheritance in his holy people,

  19 and **His incomparably great power for us who believe**. That power is the **same** as the mighty strength

  20 He exerted when He raised Christ from the dead and **seated Him at His right hand** in the heavenly realms,

  21 **far above all rule and authority, power and dominion, and every name that is invoked**, not only in the present age but also in the one to come.

  22 And God placed **all things** under His feet and appointed Him to be head over **everything** for the church,

  23 which is His body, the fullness of Him who fills **everything in every way**" (continued in the next chapter…)

- Ephesians 2:1-10 NIV:

  1 As for you, you were dead in your transgressions and sins, 2 in which you used to live when you followed the ways of this world and of the ruler of the kingdom of the air, the spirit who is now at work in those who are disobedient.

  3 All of us also lived among them at one time, gratifying the cravings of our flesh and following its desires and thoughts. Like the rest, we were by nature deserving of wrath.

  4 But because of His great love for us, God, who is rich in mercy,

5 made us alive with Christ even when we were dead in transgressions—it is by grace you have been saved.

6 And God raised us up with Christ and seated us <u>with Him</u> in the heavenly realms in Christ Jesus,

7 in order that in the coming ages he might show the incomparable riches of his grace, expressed in his kindness to us in Christ Jesus.

8 For it is by grace you have been saved, through faith—and this is not from yourselves, it is the gift of God—

9 not by works, so that no one can boast.

10 For we are God's handiwork, **created in Christ Jesus to do good works,** which God prepared **in advance for us to do.**

To further continue helping us to make the mental transition in our understanding of the total and complete nature of our authority in Christ to do the exact same works that He did, the following scripture passage provides us with an insightful, <u>behind-the-scenes view of how our enemy views the total authority in Christ that is ours</u>:

- Acts 19:13-17 NIV:

  13 Some Jews who went around driving out evil spirits tried to invoke the name of the Lord Jesus over those who were demon-possessed. They would say, "In the name of the Jesus whom Paul preaches, I command you to come out."

  14 Seven sons of Sceva, a Jewish chief priest, were doing this.

  15 One day the evil spirit answered them, **'Jesus I know, and Paul I know about, but who are you?'** *(NLT: "I know Jesus, **and I know Paul**, but who are you?")*

  16 Then the man who had the evil spirit jumped on them and overpowered them all. He gave them such a beating that they ran out of the house naked and bleeding.

With prayerful thought, the above scripture passage should make it clear that individually *we* each have the same source of power and authority that Jesus did… but only and solely in the name and authority of Jesus – no more, and no less. Although Jesus is not in bodily human form here on earth anymore, *we* are – in fact, that is why we are here…. and in His Name, we can do the same miracles that He did, and even greater, just as Jesus told us to do.

So… because our Lord Jesus has all authority here on earth, so also do we here *using His Name:*

- John 14:12,13 NIV (Jesus):
  12 Very truly I tell you, whoever believes in me will do the works I have been doing, and they will do even greater things than these, because I am going to the Father.
  13 And I will do whatever you ask **in my name**, so that the Father may be glorified in the Son.
  14 You may ask me for anything **in my name**, and I will do it.

- John 16:26-27 NIV (Jesus):
  26 In that day you will ask **in my name**. I am not saying that I will ask the Father on your behalf.
  27 No, the Father himself loves you because you have loved me and have believed that I came from God.

- Matthew 18:18 NIV (Jesus):
  Truly I tell you, **whatever you bind <u>on earth</u>** will be bound in heaven, and **whatever you loose <u>on earth</u>** will be loosed in heaven.

Finally, here is our authority on earth in action:

- Matthew 28:18-20 NLT:
  18 Jesus came and told his disciples, 'I have been given **all authority** in heaven and on earth.
  19 **Therefore**, go and make disciples of all the nations, baptizing them in the name of the Father and the Son and the Holy Spirit.
  20 Teach these new disciples to obey all the commands I have given you. And be sure of this: I am with you always, even to the end of the age.'

- Mark 16:15-20 NIV (Jesus):
  15 He said to them, '**Go into all the world** and preach the gospel to all creation.
  16 Whoever believes and is baptized will be saved, but whoever does not believe will be condemned.
  17 **And these signs will accompany those who believe**: **In my name** they will drive out demons; they will speak in new tongues;

18 they will pick up snakes with their hands; and when they drink deadly poison, it will not hurt them at all; **they will place their hands on sick people, and they will get well.'**

<u>Summary</u>: the *words "In the name of Jesus"* should mean incredibly more now than they ever have before. We can do **the same works** here on earth that Jesus did, using His Name (translation: *acting in Jesus' place).* Just wow again!

This leads us to a breathtaking reality. Based on the scriptures we have studied today, now you are ready for our memorable class motto:

"If Jesus did it, I can do it."

We understand if our class motto may sound "aggressively bold" to you at first. However, based on John 14:12, this is the Bible truth straight from the mouth of our Savior Jesus Christ Himself!

There are *separate sets of scriptures* to consider here. Yes, Jesus gave us complete authority over the works of Satan *(anything to do with Satan, including sickness, poverty, lack, etc.).* However, Jesus never gave us authority to bless ourselves with the things we need. **Instead, we must ask God the Father to bless us in Jesus' Name, and then it is totally up to the Father to say yes, no, or wait.**

2.3.3 Foundational Truth #3 of 3: How Do I Use My Authority?

Okay class, here is a question for you: Are you ready to talk to inanimate objects such as trees, the wind, body parts, cancer, fevers, and broken bones?

(show of hands!)

It is time for us to learn to speak directly to the problems we face, just as Jesus did, using His name. Let us start in the Old Testament of the Bible:

- Ezekiel 37:1-14 NIV:
  1 The hand of the Lord was on me, a. He brought me out by the Spirit of the Lord and set me in the middle of a valley; it was full of bones.

2 He led me back and forth among them, and I saw a great many bones on the floor of the valley, bones that were very dry.

3 He asked me, 'Son of man, can these bones live?'

I said, 'Sovereign Lord, you alone know.'

4 Then he said to me, 'Prophesy **to these bones** and say **to them**, '**Dry bones, hear** the word of the Lord!

5 This is what the Sovereign Lord says **to these bones**: I will make breath enter **you**, and **you** will come to life.

6 I will attach tendons to **you** and make flesh come upon **you** and cover **you** with skin; I will put breath in **you**, and **you** will come to life. Then **you** will know that I am the Lord.'

7 **So I prophesied as I was commanded.** And as I was prophesying, there was a noise, a rattling sound, and the bones came together, bone to bone.

8 I looked, and tendons and flesh appeared on them and skin covered them, but there was no breath in them.

9 Then He said to me, 'Prophesy **to the breath**; prophesy, son of man, and say **to it**, "This is what the Sovereign Lord says: **Come, breath**, from the four winds and breathe into these slain, that they may live."'

10 **So I prophesied as he commanded me**, and breath entered them; they came to life and stood up on their feet—a vast army.

- Luke 4:38-39 NIV:

  38 Jesus left the synagogue and went to the home of Simon. Now Simon's mother-in-law was suffering from a high fever, and they asked Jesus to help her.

  39 So he bent over her and **rebuked the fever**, and it left her. She got up at once and began to wait on them.

My… speaking to bones, breath, and fevers. Now it is time to talk to severe weather, trees, and fevers[7]:

---

[7] In 1 Kings 13:1-2 a prophet of God talks directly to a stone altar.

- Mark 4:37-41 NIV:

35 That day when evening came, he said to his disciples, 'Let us go over to the other side.'

36 Leaving the crowd behind, they took him along, just as he was, in the boat. There were also other boats with him.

37 A furious squall came up, and the waves broke over the boat, so that it was nearly swamped.

38 Jesus was in the stern, sleeping on a cushion. The disciples woke him and said to him, 'Teacher, don't you care if we drown?'

39 He got up, rebuked **the wind** and said **to the waves**, 'Quiet! Be still!' Then the wind died down and it was completely calm.

40 He said to his disciples, 'Why are you so afraid? Do you still have no faith?'

41 They were terrified and asked each other, 'Who is this? Even the wind and the waves obey him!'

- Mark 11:12-14, 20-25 NIV:

12 The next day as they were leaving Bethany, Jesus was hungry.

13 Seeing in the distance a fig tree in leaf, he went to find out if it had any fruit. When he reached it, he found nothing but leaves, because it was not the season for figs.

14 Then he said **to the tree**, 'May no one ever eat fruit from **you** again.' And his disciples heard him say it.

[..]

19 When evening came, Jesus and his disciples went out of the city.

20 In the morning, as they went along, they saw the fig tree withered from the roots.

21 Peter remembered and said to Jesus, 'Rabbi, look! The fig tree you cursed has withered!'

22 'Have faith in God,' Jesus answered.

23 'Truly I tell you, if anyone says **to this mountain**, "Go, throw yourself into the sea," and does not doubt in their heart but believes that what they say will happen, it will be done for them.

24 Therefore I tell you, whatever you ask for in prayer, **believe that you have received it, and it will be yours.**

25 And when you stand praying, if you hold anything against anyone, forgive them, so that your Father in heaven may forgive you your sins.'

Summary: We cannot ask God to do what He told us to do. Since Jesus gave us His authority to do signs, wonders, and miracles, then in obedience we use our authority in Christ to speak directly to the problems and obstacles of our enemy that are in our way, using the name of Jesus (acting in His place).

2.4 Conditions Apply When Healing Christians

Before you pray for the healing of a <u>Christian</u> believer, be aware that important conditions apply from scripture which must adhered to for a miracle to occur. A short preview of these important conditions follows next.

Note: a detailed study of these conditions will occur over the remainder of this 10-week class series.

2.4.1 Faith Confession

When a Christian believer needs healing, it is critical to make sure that the believer's faith confession is right before you pray for their healing. Here is an example from the healing ministry of Jesus, our example:

- Mark 9:22-24 NLT:
  22 'The (evil) spirit often throws (this father's son) into the fire or into water, trying to kill him. Have mercy on us and help us, if you can.'
  23 **'What do you mean, "If I can?"'** Jesus asked. 'Anything is possible if a person believes.'
  24 The father instantly cried out, 'I do believe, but help me overcome my unbelief!'

We will learn many more important details about this topic later in this 10-week class.

_____

_____

_____

2.4.2 We Must Demonstrate Our Faith By Our Actions

Here is a major condition to the physical healing of ourselves and our fellow Christian believers that does **not** apply to non-believers:

- James 2:26 KJV: Faith without works is dead.

From much experience based on the words of Jesus in Mark 11:24 NIV (quoted on the prior page and again on the following page), your class instructors have observed that only about 10% of Christians in each church who need physical healing will be prophetically singled out and healed by the sovereign will of the Holy Spirit. This type of healing requires little or no faith on the part of the receiver (next week we will carefully examine Acts 3:1-10 to fully understand this type of healing).

However, the remainder (~90%) of Christians in each church who need physical healing must be willing to stand on their own faith if they are to receive the miracle they need. This means being properly prayed by a Christian believer and then actively demonstrate their faith by *speaking* and *acting* on their faith that he or she has been healed, which then results in their healing.

The quickest way healings by faith occur is if the person doing the praying uses the following approach:

1) Quote relevant scriptures about the situation;
2) Testify of his/her own of healing (as may be applicable), and;
3) Speak and acts in bold faith derived from the Word of God.

This helps to raise the faith of the Christian believer recipients to believe God's Word for themselves so they can receive their healing.

We will learn many more significant details about this important subject later in this 10-week class.

_____

_____

_____

_____

2.4.3. We Must Forgive In Order To Be Healed

In the context of Biblical healing, notice again the instructions of Jesus in this previously quoted scripture passage in this lesson (see above):

- Mark 11:12-14, 20-25 NIV (Jesus:
  24 Therefore I tell you, whatever you ask for in prayer, believe that you have received it, and it will be yours.
  25 And when you stand praying, **if you hold anything against anyone, forgive them,** so that your Father in heaven may forgive you your sins.'

We will learn much more about this incredibly important subject later in this 10-week class.

2.5 Illustrative Testimonies

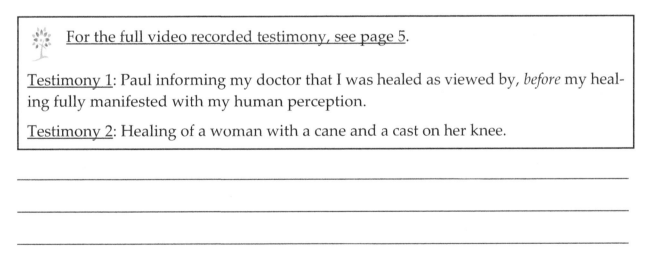

For the full video recorded testimony, see page 5.

Testimony 1: Paul informing my doctor that I was healed as viewed by, *before* my healing fully manifested with my human perception.

Testimony 2: Healing of a woman with a cane and a cast on her knee.

_____

_____

_____

<u>Testimony 3</u>: Healing of Michelle's painful hip joints.

_____

_____

_____

2.6 Coming Up Next Week

As a preview, we will learn important practical applications of this lesson when class instructors Brian and Paul relate their powerful testimony in our next lesson entitled, *"Using Our Authority in Christ in Real Life."*

Additional Class Notes *(Lesson Two)*

Your Personal Notes, Observations and Class Activities:

_____

_____

_____

_____

_____

_____

_____

_____

_____

_____

_____

_____

_____

_____

_____

_____

_____

_____

_____

Unresolved questions you may have for your additional study over the remainder of this book:

1. _____

_____

_____

_____

_____

_____

2. _____

_____

_____

_____

_____

3. _____

_____

_____

_____

_____

2.7 Walking It Out – Class Assignment (LESSON TWO)

WALKING IT OUT Class Assignment (LESSON TWO)

<u>OUR ACTION PLAN</u>

<u>*Seek* **JESUS** at a *level and depth that you may not have previously to* continually further develop and deepen your intimate, personal relationship with Jesus.</u>

Continued Class Action Assignments

Read Daily: "Expect to Believe: 90 Bible Devotionals to Grow Your Faith for the Impossible" by Paul Williams *(expect a close encounter with the Holy Spirit to happen while reading these devotionals daily).*

Watch / Listen to the Class Lesson Videos; pause when needed to read-pray scriptures, work Action Plan steps, work Homework Challenges and Go Deeper **as** you go through your class notes AGAIN (including *journaling revelations the Holy Spirit has shown you).*

Review Weekly: Key Learning Objectives *(check off each one as you achieve the objectives of this week's lesson (see this chapter's Introduction). Ask the Holy Spirit to plant these objectives deep in your heart and mind and help put them into practice in your daily life.*

Suggested Action: engage in a fast to help create an intimate relationship with God *(per section 1.2 apply the three key takeaways that the author learned).* God responds to those who seek Him through fasting and prayer. <u>***Adding a Biblically based food-fast is even better and can aid in combination with God's Word and prayer to a significant breakthrough*** </u>*(see section 1.12).* <u>**Speak aloud** the action items in the seven steps taken from **James 4:7-10**,</u> *especially steps 5 & 6 (see section 1.12).*

Daily abide in the overflow of the anointing of Holy Spirit *(as described in sections 1.5 and 1.6).* Ask the Holy Spirit **every day** to **soften your heart and fill you with God's amazing love** for Your fellow created human beings. Re-commit to earnestly seeking the Holy Ghost in His fullness in your life.

Daily read and apply the books of _John, Acts, and Ephesians_[8] *(see section 1.12)* using the "read-pray the Word approach" and the "Seven Steps to Intimate Relationship with God."

Ask the Holy Spirit to guard your mouth and direct your path. Focus on speaking what the Holy Spirit leads you to say, going where the Holy Spirit directs you to go, and doing what the Holy Spirit says to do.

Action Assignments for Lesson Two

Review Lesson One Homework Challenge and Going Deeper to make sure you have attained them in your daily walk.

Review and Practice to learn the weekly objectives for this week's class *(see section 2.1)*

Learn and know (absorb, understand, and live) the three important foundational truths from God's Word. *(see section 2.3)*

Review and learn the important conditions which Christians must adhere to, in order to receive their miracle *(see section 2.4.1, 2.4.2 and 2.4.3)*

Read-Pray the scriptures daily *(see section 2.3.3, also 2.4.1 – 2.4.3)*

Speak directly to the problems you face, just as Jesus did, using His Name.

HOMEWORK CHALLENGE

1. What is our class motto?

_____

_____

---

[8] In our observation, no other combination of three books in the Bible gives as much spiritual return for the time expended. These three books serve as an effective jumping point to real-pray the remainder of the entire Bible.

2. What can we NOT ask God to do? Also, why not?

_____

_____

_____

_____

_____

_____

3. What is the healing commission that Jesus gave believers in Him?

_____

_____

_____

_____

_____

4. The three foundational truths as discussed in this chapter are:

_____

_____

_____

_____

_____

_____

5. When did Jesus start doing healing? _____

_____

_____

6. How did Jesus heal? _____

_____

7. Where does the root source of our authority lie?

_____

_____

_____

_____

8. How does the enemy view the total authority in Christ that is ours? (Acts 19:13-17)

_____

_____

_____

_____

9. When was our authority on earth put into action? What did Jesus say that confirms our authority?

_____

_____

_____

10. Before you pray for healing of a Christian, what are several important conditions which apply from scripture, which must be adhered to for a miracle to occur?

_____

_____

_____

_____

_____

_____

11. What is suppressed healing? *(review class lesson video)*

_____

_____

_____

_____

12. A Christian needing physical healing must be willing to stand on their own faith to receive the miracle they need. What does this mean?

_____

_____

_____

_____

_____

13. What are the three quickest ways to raise the faith of a Christian believer to believe God's Word for themselves, so they can receive their healing?

_____

_____

_____

_____

_____

14. When a Christian Believer needs healing it is critical to make sure the believer's _____ is right before you pray for healing?

15. What type of healing requires little or no faith in the recipient?

_____

_____

_____

_____

16. Explain the major condition to the physical healing of believers, which does NOT apply to non-believers:

_____

_____

_____

_____

_____

_____

17. What is real forgiveness per Mark 11:12-14, 20-25?

_____

_____

_____

_____

18. If you have been watching the free companion video instruction to this book (see page 5), then by now you have watched initial examples of how to pray for and witness to unbelievers such as atheists. What is common throughout these examples?

_____

_____

_____

_____

_____

_____

GOING DEEPER (Journal Time)

1. Just how pure and perfect was the sacrifice Jesus did for us? Does this open your mind and change your thinking about who you are in Christ, the authority you have, and how you can use your authority?

_____

_____

2. Who **am** I in Christ? Do **I believe** I have Christ given authority?

_____

_____

3. Meditate and journal on John 17:22-23 in several different translations, then decide what this means to you.

_____

_____

4. What was the attitude of Christ Jesus in Philippians 2:5-8 that we must also have?

_____

_____

5. What do the words **"in the name of Jesus"** mean to you? Has the meaning of these word changed for you since the start of this class? If so, in what way(s)?

_____

_____

6. How can you physically heal the sick and injured on the spot like Jesus did? What have you learned so far and what do you need to learn to now start applying to your thinking, life and walk to begin to accomplish on the spot healings?

_____

_____

7. Ask the Holy Spirit to direct you to places where you can go and to people you are to pray for. Remember what the author said about unbelievers and new Christians.

Encouragement: Do not be concerned about making a mistake. Your faith will continue to increase as you continue to practice and begin to achieve results.

3

Using Our Authority in Christ in Real Life

CLASS TESTIMONIES FROM the past week:

_____

_____

_____

_____

Here are our learning objectives for Lesson 3:

- Understand the differences between two very different types of physical healing.

- Learn how to apply our authority in Christ in difficult, real-world field situations.

3.1 Two Types of Physical Healings

In preparation for our illustrative testimony from Zambia, Africa, it is important to know that there are two distinctly different types of miracles which apply to Christians only, not unbelievers.

The first and most common type can be called, _Healing by Faith_ (applicable to about 90% of all Christians who need physical healing), while the second can be called, _Healing by the Will of the Holy Spirit_ (applicable to about 10% of all Christians who need physical healing).

Here are the key differences between these two distinct types of healing miracles:

- **Type 1 - Healing by Faith:** in this method, faith –in the form of *words* and *action* —is required on the part of the Christian believer who is receiving the miracle. Here is an example from the Bible:

    o Matthew 9:20,21 NIV:

      20 Just then a woman who had been subject to bleeding for twelve years came up behind him and touched the edge of his cloak.

      21 She said to herself, **'If I only touch his cloak, I will be healed.'**

      22 Jesus turned and saw her. 'Take heart, daughter,' he said, **'your faith has healed you.'** And the woman was healed at that moment.

- **Type 2 - Healing by the Will of the Holy Spirit:** in this method, typically little or no faith is required on the part of the person receiving the miracle. Here is an example in the Bible:

- Acts 3:1-8 NIV:

  3 One day Peter and John were going up to the temple at the time of prayer — at three in the afternoon.

  2 Now a man who was lame from birth was being carried to the temple gate called Beautiful, where he was put every day to beg from those going into the temple courts.

  3 When he saw Peter and John about to enter, **he asked them for money.**

  4 Peter looked straight at him, as did John. Then Peter said, 'Look at us!'

  5 So the man gave them his attention, **expecting to get something from them.**

  6 Then Peter said, 'Silver or gold I do not have, **but what I do have I give you. In the name of Jesus Christ of Nazareth, walk.'**

  7 Taking him by the right hand, he helped him up, and instantly the man's feet and ankles became strong.

  8 He jumped to his feet and began to walk. Then he went with them into the temple courts, walking and jumping, and praising God.

The Holy Spirit is our Advocate, Teacher, Comforter, Guide, and the source of our Power (John 16:7-15 and Acts 1:8 quoted in this lesson previously). **The Holy Spirit's leading** in every situation we encounter **must always supersede all plans we may have.**

3.2 God Saves a Nation: The Story of Zambia, Africa

 For the full video recorded testimony, see page 5.

Let us apply what we learned so far in Lessons 1 and 2 in this class series to a real-life business trip to a foreign country in a distant continent.

Testimony: *"Lessons from Zambia, Africa: Learning to Pray Effectively for Signs, Wonders and Miracles"* is the story of how your class instructors Brian and Paul met and began working together, first in ministry and later in business. In the process, God saved the nation of Zambia using these two, as his vessels to accomplish multiple miracles.

Background Information -- Paul's July 2015 Trip to Zambia, Africa:
https://youtu.be/MYCrVfRLVdU
(9 minutes 30 seconds)

Testimony Outline

- Short notice calls to Washington, DC

- Paul mistakes the purpose of this trip, and God uses a stranger at the time – class instructor Brian Desilets — to fix this error.

- Prayer, fasting and a hasty departure for Zambia, Africa

- God heals a chronically blind evangelist pastor on the plane.

- 46-hour marathon trip via Nigeria and South Africa to Zambia

- Surprise! A lovely, clean super-majority Christian nation (95.5% Christian per Wikipedia as of July 2022)

- Dealing with filthy water and food… and then disease-filled mosquitos.

- Gray hair galore, oh my!

- A big problem is discovered in Zambia that threatens the livelihoods and economic prosperity of the nation.

- 3:00 AM wake-up call in Houston wins the victory from 7,000 miles away.

- Critical presentation to the Zambia government

- Shocking surprise: God saves the nation of Zambia from disaster.

Paul's first two "disciples" in Zambia

- Paul's final day in Zambia: a tiny mistake in his earlier prayer request exacts a real but humorous cost upon his departure.

- Discipling the nation using their cab drivers

- God uses the gift of prophecy and an incredible miracle through a stubborn, hard-headed atheist to turn Zambia's food exports around.

Now, for the stunning indirect aftermath three months later: on October 18, 2015, over 1 million Zambians from across the nation led by their President gathered outdoors to solemnly observe the *"Day of National Repentance, Prayer and Fasting."*

Over 1 million Zambian led by their President Edgar Lungu
fast, repent, and pray and seek God's blessing

Surprise!

Key takeaway lessons from the story of Zambia, Africa: (see the full video recorded testimony).

3.3 Final Reminder for the Class Assignment:

The Holy Spirit's instructions and guidance will *always* align with scripture or point us to scripture. Remember – we will only notice error if we are well-versed in God's Word sufficiently enough to know the difference. After all, Satan had the audacity to mis-quote scripture to Jesus its author, so obviously the devil can and will mis-quote scripture to us as well as those we are praying for, too.

Finally, if there ever is a variance between God's Word and the guidance you are receiving from what you believe is the Holy Spirit, *then the guidance you are receiving is **not from God**!* If this occurs, immediately seek the prayerful assistance of Godly leaders who adhere closely to the full gospel of God's Word.

God bless you to apply what you have learned throughout this coming week!

Additional Class Notes (Lesson Three)

Your Personal Notes, Observations, and Class Activities

_____

_____

_____

_____

_____

_____

_____

_____

_____

_____

_____

_____

_____

_____

_____

_____

_____

_____

_____

_____

_____

Questions for the Instructors or the class:

1. _____

_____

_____

_____

_____

2. _____

_____

_____

_____

_____

3. _____

_____

_____

_____

_____

3.4 Walking It Out – Class Assignment (LESSON THREE)

WALKING IT OUT Class Assignment (LESSON THREE)

OUR ACTION PLAN

Seek **JESUS** at a *level and depth that you may not have previously to* continually further develop and deepen your intimate, personal relationship with Jesus.

Continued Class Action Assignments

Read Daily: "Expect to Believe: 90 Bible Devotionals to Increase Your Faith for the Impossible" by Paul Williams *(expect a close encounter with the Holy Spirit to happen while reading these devotionals daily).*

Watch / Listen to the Class Lesson Videos; pause when needed to read-pray scriptures, work Action Plan steps, work Homework Challenges, and Go Deeper **as** you go through your class notes *(journal revelations Holy Spirit has shown you).*

Review Weekly: Key Learning Objectives *(check off each one as you achieve the objectives of this week's lesson (see this chapter's Introduction). Ask the Holy Spirit to plant these objectives deep in your heart and mind and help put them into practice in your daily life.*

Suggested Action: fast, creating an intimate relationship with God: *(per section 1.2 apply the three key takeaways that the author learned).* God responds to fasting and prayer. ***Adding a Biblically based food-fast is even better and can aid in combination with God's Word and prayer to a significant breakthrough*** *(see section 1.12)* ***Speak aloud** the action items in the seven steps taken from **James 4:7-10** (especially steps 5& 6 (see section 1.12)).*

Daily abide in the overflow of the anointing of Holy Spirit *(as described in sections 1.5 and 1.6).* Ask the Holy Spirit **every day** to **soften your heart and fill you with God's amazing love** for Your fellow created human beings. Re-commit to earnestly seeking the Holy Ghost in His fullness in your life.

Daily read and apply the books of _John, Acts, and Ephesians_[9] *(see section 1.12)* using the "read-pray the Word approach" and the "Seven Steps to Intimate Relationship with God."

Ask the Holy Spirit to guard your mouth and direct your path throughout each day.

Action Assignments for Lesson Three →

Review Lesson One and Two action steps to make sure you have attained them in your daily walk.

Try your absolute best to put into practice the admonishment of the apostle Paul in this scripture passage:

- Ephesians 6:18 NLT:
  Pray in the Spirit at all times and on every occasion. Stay alert and be persistent in your prayers for all believers everywhere.

During your prayer time, ask God to help you overcome your doubts about yourself praying for strangers as He increases the love in your heart for the lost and hurting. *Ask Him to help you remove all blocks* keeping you from following His commission.

Start boldly sharing the truth you are learning in class and during your read-pray times with friends and family around you. This will help you absorb what you are reading and build your faith …. *From the mouth your heart will speak*!

Always remember that divine healing and the casting out demons do not work by the application of formulas – rather, <u>we must follow Jesus' example in scripture,</u> while at the same time <u>actively seeking for and listening to the case-by-case prophetic inspiration of the Holy Spirit</u>

---

[9] In our observation, no other combination of three books in the Bible gives as much spiritual return for the time expended. These three books serve as an effective jumping point to read-pray the remainder of the entire Bible.

> **Remember: The Holy Spirit's instructions and guidance** will *always* directly point us to scripture or align closely with scripture. *This is another important reason why our goal should be to become well-versed in God's Word.*

HOMEWORK CHALLENGE

1. What are the two distinctly different types of healing miracles called?

_____

_____

2. _____ requires the Christian believer who is receiving the miracle to have faith and is ____% of all Christians who need healing.

3. Healing by _____ typically requires little or no faith on the part of the person receiving the miracle and is about _____% of all Christians who need healing.

4. The Holy Spirit is our _____ , _____, _____, _____ and source of our power. (*see John 16:7-15 and Acts 1:8*)

5. Make a list of the tough times the author faced and how the Holy Spirit protected him and or moved.

_____

_____

_____

_____

_____

6. When we (*our mind / spirit*) receive instructions we only notice an error if we are _____ _____ enough to know the difference.

_____

_____

GOING DEEPER (Journal Time)

1. Review lessons from the Zambia Testimony outline in section 5.2. Reflect on what all you learned about how the Holy Spirit worked to save a nation. What is your personal takeaway from the testimony?

_____

_____

2. What facts about Zambia did you learn as a Godly Nation? How did one area of faith with no action almost ruin their nation?

_____

_____

3. What happened on the National Day of Repentance and Fasting on October 18, 2015 in Zambia that inspired you? How could you pray for this to happen in the country live in now?

4. Ask God to prepare the hearts of the people you will be praying for as He prepares you to go forth. Make a list of all the places that come to your mind. Be praying for these places and be prepared to go whenever the Holy Spirit leads. Expect God to Move! Remember the prayers of the author in Zambia required him to show his faith with his actions.

_____

_____

4

Casting Out Demons The Way Jesus Did

CLASS TESTIMONIES FROM the past week:

_____

_____

_____

_____

Here are our learning objectives for Lesson 4:

- Learn to let the Holy Spirit lead as we minister to others.

- Understand the enormous power that God's Word has on our enemy.

- Learn how to discern the presence of evil spirits which are _oppressing_ or _possessing_ their victims (two different meanings).

- Learn how to cast out evil spirits, and…

- Learn how to prevent demons from returning to their victims.

4.1 The Perils of Formulaic Thinking

It is critical that we do not fall into formulaic thinking in our prayers for the sick and demon possessed. Because of our important second lesson in this book on our authority in Christ (_"Who I am, What do I have, and How do I use it"_), it can be all-too-easy for us to focus on doctrine, tactics and the mechanics associated with healing while meanwhile inadvertently losing sight of the Person of Jesus and His tangible Presence and anointing in the form and power of the Holy Spirit our Teacher and Guide who lives within us.

When this occurs, our ability to do miracles will lessen and then stop (although we can generally still help others to be healed by raising *their* faith for their healing).

So, let us review the scriptures to gain an important reminder that the source of our power is the mighty Holy Spirit.

———————————————————————————————————

———————————————————————————————————

———————————————————————————————————

———————————————————————————————————

4.2 Let the Holy Spirit Take the Lead

Let us begin examining this important topic by taking a close look at how Jesus as our example healed four different blind men in four completely different ways:

- Luke 18:35-43 NIV:
  35 As Jesus approached Jericho, a blind man was sitting by the roadside begging.
  36 When he heard the crowd going by, he asked what was happening.
  37 They told him, 'Jesus of Nazareth is passing by.'
  38 He called out, 'Jesus, Son of David, have mercy on me!'
  39 Those who led the way rebuked him and told him to be quiet, but he shouted all the more, 'Son of David, have mercy on me!'
  40 Jesus stopped and ordered the man to be brought to him. When he came near, Jesus asked him,
  41 'What do you want me to do for you?' 'Lord, I want to see,' he replied.
  42 Jesus **said to him**, 'Receive your sight; your faith has healed you.'
  43 Immediately he received his sight and followed Jesus, praising God. When all the people saw it, they also praised God.

- Matthew 9:27-31 NIV:
  27 As Jesus went on from there, two blind men followed him, calling out, "Have mercy on us, Son of David!"
  28 When he had gone indoors, the blind men came to him, and he asked them, "Do you believe that I am able to do this?"
  "Yes, Lord," they replied.

29 **Then he touched their eyes and said**, "According to your faith let it be done to you";

30 **and their sight was restored.** Jesus warned them sternly, "See that no one knows about this."

31 But they went out and spread the news about him all over that region.

- Mark 8:22-25 NIV:

  22 They came to Bethsaida, and some people brought a blind man and begged Jesus to touch him.

  23 He took the blind man by the hand and led him outside the village. When **he had spit on the man's eyes and put his hands on him**, Jesus asked, 'Do you see anything?'

  24 He looked up and said, 'I see people; they look like trees walking around.'

  25 **Once more Jesus put his hands on the man's eyes.** Then his eyes were opened, his sight was restored, and he saw everything clearly.

- John 9:1-7 NIV:

  1 As he went along, he saw a man blind from birth.

  2 His disciples asked him, 'Rabbi, who sinned, this man or his parents, that he was born blind?'

  3 'Neither this man nor his parents sinned,' said Jesus, 'but this happened so that the works of God might be displayed in him.

  4 As long as it is day, we must do the works of him who sent me. Night is coming, when no one can work.

  5 While I am in the world, I am the light of the world.'

  6 After saying this, **he spit on the ground, made some mud with the saliva, and put it on the man's eyes.**

  7 'Go,' he told him, **'wash in the Pool of Siloam'** (this word means "Sent"). **So the man went and washed and came home seeing.**

So why did Jesus heal four separate cases of the same physical condition (blind eyes) in four completely different ways? Why didn't Jesus heal all four blind men in the same way?

Answer: Jesus healed only as He was so led and directed by the Holy Spirit[10]. We clearly see this in scripture:

---

[10] According to 1 Corinthians 12:9 (NIV), the Holy Spirit gives "gift<u>s</u> *(plural)* of healing," not "the gift *(singular)* of healing." We will learn about this subject in chapter 7.

- Isaiah 11:1-3 NIV:
  1 A shoot will come up from the stump of Jesse; from his roots a Branch will bear fruit.
  2 **The Spirit of the Lord will rest on him— the Spirit of wisdom and of understanding, the Spirit of counsel and of might,** the Spirit of the knowledge and fear of the Lord—
  3 and he will delight in the fear of the Lord. He will not judge by what he sees with his eyes, or decide by what he hears with his ears;

- John 3:34 NIV:
  For he (Jesus) is sent by God. He speaks God's words, **for God gives him the Spirit without limit.**

- John 5:19, 20 NIV:
  19 Jesus gave them this answer: 'Very truly I tell you, **the Son can do nothing by himself; he can do only what he sees his Father doing,** because whatever the Father does the Son also does.
  20 For the Father loves the Son **and shows him all he does.** Yes, and he will show him even greater works than these, so that you will be amazed.'

- John 14:10 NIV (Jesus):
  Don't you believe that I am in the Father, and that the Father is in me? The words I say to you I do not speak on my own authority. **Rather, it is the Father, living in me, who is doing his work.**

Because Jesus lived as a man here on earth as we learned in lessons 1 and 2, He knew from much first-person experience exactly how the Father goes about communicating His instructions to us through the mediation of the Holy Spirit:

- John 14:26 NIV (Jesus):
  But the Advocate, the Holy Spirit, whom the Father will send in my name, **will teach you all things and will remind you of everything I have said to you.**

- John 16:13, 14 NIV (Jesus):
  13 But when he, the Spirit of truth, comes, **he will guide you into all the truth. He will not speak on his own; he will speak only what he hears, and he will tell you what is yet to come.**

14 He will glorify me because it is **from me** that he will receive what he will make known to you.

- Romans 8:26 NIV:

  26 In the same way, the Spirit helps us in our weakness. **We do not know what we ought to pray for, but the Spirit himself intercedes for us through wordless groans.**

  27 And he who searches our hearts knows the mind of the Spirit, because the Spirit intercedes for God's people in accordance with the will of God.

- Romans 8:5, 14 NIV:

  5 Those who live according to the flesh have their minds set on what the flesh desires; **but those who live in accordance with the Spirit have their minds set on what the Spirit desires.**

  [...]

  14 For those who are led by the Spirit of God are the children of God.

Just as the Holy Spirit led Jesus during His earthly ministry here on earth living as a man, so also will the Holy Spirit lead us as we seek His presence and leading in all we do.

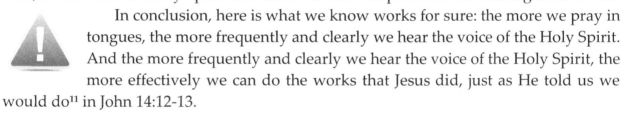

In conclusion, here is what we know works for sure: the more we pray in tongues, the more frequently and clearly we hear the voice of the Holy Spirit. And the more frequently and clearly we hear the voice of the Holy Spirit, the more effectively we can do the works that Jesus did, just as He told us we would do[11] in John 14:12-13.

_____

_____

_____

4.3 How To Cast Out Demons Using Jesus' Name

So, are you ready to learn how to cast out demons? Let's get started!

_____

[11] Excepted from Lesson 90 in "Expect to Believe: 90 Bible Devotionals to Increase Your Faith for the Impossible."

4.3.1 Dealing With Abnormal Fear or Apprehension

Before we continue any further, are any of you experiencing abnormally strong feelings of fear and/or apprehension? Or do any of you have a sudden powerful urge to end this Bible Study or go do something else? If so, please take the small but bold –and important-- step of faith by raising your hand or asking someone with you for prayer.

Similarly, if such feelings hit as this class continues tonight, ask for help without hesitation. We all have been there, including your class instructors. So, we well-understand from an ample amount of personal experience how to help and not question or judge!

As soon as you raise your hand, your class instructors will immediately stop and pray for you in the name of Jesus. Your fear and apprehension will leave immediately. (If you are in a remote class with others, ask others to pray in faith for the spirit of fear to leave).

(class prayer)

_____

_____

_____

_____

4.3.2 Class Poll

Let us take a class poll. Get ready to vote!

Here we go. If you are a student of this class who has never cast a demon out before <u>by yourself</u> – not as part of a collaborative effort of a group – then this poll is for you. If this is you and you have participated in this class from the beginning and you now fully know, understand and have fully absorbed into your spirit and soul <u>everything</u> that has taught in this class series to far, including *Who* you are in Christ, *What* authority you have, and *How* to Use it, what do you think would most likely happen if you were to encounter a demon-possessed person right now and you commanded the evil spirit(s) to leave in the mighty name of Jesus?

Class poll choices:

A. The demon(s) will leave.
B. The demon(s) will not only refuse to leave, but will argue with you, curse you and fight you.

Answer: {to be provided by your class instructors[12]}

4.3.3 Taking Authority Over Evil Spirits

It is worth noting that many Christians who know who they are in Christ, know their authority in Christ, and know how to use it nevertheless still find it difficult, frightening, and oh-so-time consuming to cast out demons, if the demons ever leave at all. Obviously, something is very wrong! Clearly, we need to learn what the problem is quickly so we can fix it, and fast.

Let us start by understanding that the problem definitely <u>is not</u> Jesus or His all-powerful name. To recap from the scriptures, there is absolute power in His name as given Him by the Father, as we read here:

- Philippians 2:9 NIV:
  9 Therefore **God exalted (Jesus) to the highest place** and gave him the name that is above every name,
  10 that at the name of Jesus **every knee should bow**, in heaven and on earth and under the earth,
  11 and **every tongue acknowledge that Jesus Christ is Lord**, to the glory of God the Father.

- James 2:19 NIV:
  You believe that there is one God. Good! **Even the demons believe that— and shudder.**

So then… if the problem is not Jesus or His mighty name, and if we fully know *Who* we are, *What* authority we have, and *How* to use it, then what in the world is the problem?

A thought – should I pray and ask God to *make* Satan obey me?

Answer: no, that will not work either! {class discussion as to why}

---

[12] See page 5 for the link to our free online companion video instruction for this book.

Okay, here is the solution: in particular when we first begin casting out demons, we must start by using the Word of God to force Satan to acknowledge our authority over him. After our complete authority over demons has been established, from that point on evil spirits will obey our commands immediately on the spot.

To help to drive home finally this powerful lesson about the enormous power of God's Word the Bible, your class instructors will use an illustrative skit.

 <u>Skit</u>: Illustration by your class instructors depicting a real-world battle over a stolen house[13] as a powerful example of why it is necessary to take authority over our enemy in order to force his compliance.

Now let us re-study the scriptures once again in two parts in order to fully this time understand the absolute power of God's Word like never before. First, a review of the power of God's Word to our lives in general:

- Hebrews 4:12 NLT: For the word of God is **alive** and **powerful**. It is sharper than the sharpest two-edged sword, cutting between soul and spirit, between joint and marrow. It exposes our innermost thoughts and desires.

- John 6:63 NLT (Jesus): The Spirit alone gives eternal life. Human effort accomplishes nothing. **And the very words I have spoken to you are spirit and life.**

- John 15:7 NLT: "**But if you remain in me and my words remain in you**, you may ask for **anything** you want, and it will be granted!"

Now, let us restudy Jesus' ministry in scripture here on earth. Acting as our example in all things, He showed us the perfect example of how to immediately break all the power of our enemy the devil:

- Matthew 4:4, 7,10, 11 NIV:
  4 Jesus answered (the devil), "It is written: 'Man shall not live on bread alone, but on every word that comes from the mouth of God'" (reference to Deut. 8:3).
  6 (The devil) said, "throw yourself down. For it is written…" (reference to Psalm 91:11,12).
  7 Jesus answered him, "It is also written: Do not put the Lord your God to the test" (reference to Deut. 6:16).

---

[13] See page 5 for the link to our free online companion video instruction for this book.

10 Jesus said to him, "Away from me, Satan! For it is written: Worship the Lord your God and serve him only" (reference to Deut. 6:13).

11 Then the devil left him, and angels came and attended him.

Satan lost the battle because he could not out-quote scripture to Jesus, who was acting in every way as a man. God's Word decides every battle in the courts of heaven and in the supernatural – for <u>both</u> sides!!! God the Father chooses to be bound (constrained) by His promises in His Powerful Word, and likewise Satan accepts God's Word on the spot *without* any question or argument!!!

Now do you finally fully understand at last why the close daily meditative study of God's Word is so EXTREMELY IMPORTANT? Hopefully you do and will take appropriate corrective action as may be necessary *(review our first class lesson again)*.

 <u>Solution</u>: Use God's Word to establish our authority over Satan, in particular during the initial battle at the beginning of your ministry. Then once you have won this battle, your use of the powerful name of Jesus and at times your re-application of appropriate scriptures as needed will quickly demolish every demonic stronghold.

Now you are just about ready to start casting out demons – and most importantly of all, doing your part to sure our enemy's former victims stay free! More is coming up next on both subjects.

———————————————————————————————————————

———————————————————————————————————————

———————————————————————————————————————

———————————————————————————————————————

4.3.4 Demons Often Cause Disease and Mental Illness

Did you know? A significant percentage (10 – 25%) of all sickness and mental illness are *not caused by* real physical problems in our bodies at all, but rather are the result of demonic attacks on the victim's body.

We can clearly see this from scripture:

- Matthew 9:32-33 NIV:

  32 While they were going out, a man who was **demon-possessed and could not talk** was brought to Jesus.

  33 **And when the demon was driven out, the man who had been mute spoke.** The crowd was amazed and said, 'Nothing like this has ever been seen in Israel.'

- Luke 13:10-17 NIV:

  10 On a Sabbath Jesus was teaching in one of the synagogues,

  11 and a woman was there who had been **crippled by a spirit** for eighteen years. She was bent over and could not straighten up at all.

  12 When Jesus saw her, he called her forward and said to her, "Woman, **you are set free** from your infirmity."

  13 Then he put his hands on her, and immediately she straightened up and praised God.

In this latter example, notice the unique wording of Jesus to the woman: *"you are set free."*

If someone is sick or injured because of the bodily oppression or possession by one or more evil spirits, in such cases your rebuke of their physical symptoms in the name of Jesus will <u>not</u> result in their healing.

Instead, an approach that generally works well is to rebuke the physical symptoms while also at the same time rebuking "any attack or plan of the evil one" against that individual.

An even better approach is to use wisdom (preferably direct prophetic discernment directly or via someone is ministering with you) to discern the specific manifestation of the evil spirit in the victim's body and then cast it out in the name of Jesus. Direct prophetic insight from the Holy Spirit is extremely powerful and should always replace any pre-planned approach of our own!

_____

_____

_____

_____

4.3.5 Casting Out Demons Like Jesus Did

Jesus had (and has) complete authority over evil spirits. So, it is no wonder that Jesus cast out demons with a simple command:

- Matthew 8:16 NIV:
  When evening came, many who were demon-possessed were brought to him, and he drove out the spirits **with a word** and healed all the sick. (NLT: "He cast out the evil spirits **with a simple command...**").

Reminder: we believers can do the same things Jesus did as stated by our Savior in His own words in John 14:12. Therefore it should be no surprise that the apostle Paul likewise ejected a demon with a single command:

- Acts 16:18 NIV:
  She (a possessed slave girl) kept (harassing Paul) for many days. Finally, Paul became so annoyed that he turned around and said to the spirit, "In the name of Jesus Christ I command you to come out of her!" **At that moment the spirit left her.**

Reminder: Jesus not only delegated His authority over demons to us, but He furthermore He *commanded* us to cast out demons:

- Matthew 10:1, 8 NIV:
  1 Jesus called his twelve disciples to him and gave them **authority to drive out impure spirits** and to heal every disease and sickness.
  [..]
  9 Heal the sick, raise the dead, cleanse those who have leprosy, **drive out demons.** Freely you have received; freely give.

 It is important to notice that Jesus did not instruct us to ask *Him* to heal the sick and drive out demons on our behalf. Rather, Jesus gave *us* (His believers) His authority to heal and cast out demons ourselves by using His name. There is a significant difference between these two ways of casting out demons! **The first approach ends in failure, while the second approach yields results.**

Huh? You might be thinking at this point, *Say what??!!! Am I supposed to cast out demons? I thought Jesus had this part covered for me!*

Answer: as already reviewed from scripture previously in this lesson, Jesus gave His authority to us to do the same things that He did here on earth, and in fact to do even greater things than He did (John 14:12). As learned in Chapter 2, *we* are the ones who are doing these miracles using the name and authority of our Lord and Savior Jesus in the power of the Holy Spirit, by speaking directly to the problems in His name. Carefully notice the instructions of Jesus about *what* (or sometimes *who* – our enemy*)* we must speak to:

- Mark 11:23 -24 NIV (Jesus):
  23 Truly I tell you, if anyone **says to this mountain**, 'Go, throw yourself into the sea,' and does not doubt in their heart but believes that what they say will happen, it will be done for them.
  24 Therefore I tell you, **whatever** you ask for in prayer, believe that you have received it, and it will be yours.

Jesus' instructions here work equally well to rebuke sickness and evil spirits alike.

As another reminder of last week's lesson, Jesus acting as a man here on earth has given *us* the ability to use the same source of power that He used, which is the mighty Holy Spirit.

With the Holy Spirit's indwelling power in abundance within the apostle Paul, no wonder the demon in this scripture passage recognized Paul's name in the context of our Christ-given authority to cast out demons:

- Acts 19:13-16 NIV:
  13 Some Jews who went around driving out evil spirits tried to invoke the name of the Lord Jesus over those who were demon-possessed. They would say, "In the name of the Jesus whom Paul preaches, I command you to come out."
  14 Seven sons of Sceva, a Jewish chief priest, were doing this.
  15 One day the evil spirit answered them, **"Jesus I know, and Paul I know about, but who are you?"**
  16 Then the man who had the evil spirit jumped on them and overpowered them all. He gave them such a beating that they ran out of the house naked and bleeding.

And as we individually so desire, we can each ask for, seek, and receive the Holy Spirit and His indwelling power just as Jesus' disciples did on the day of Pentecost in Acts chapter 2.

_____

_____

_____

_____

4.3.6 How To Prevent Demons from Returning

You will soon see from our illustrative testimonies how identifying and casting out demons is relatively straightforward.

However, preventing the demon(s) from returning to their former victims is often the hard part – in fact, at times the exceptionally hard part. We actually risk making the delivered person's situation *worse* than it was at first. This can be seen in stark warnings from Jesus and the apostle Peter in the following scripture passages:

- John 5:14 NIV:
  Later Jesus found him (a man Jesus had healed) at the temple and said to him, 'See, you are well again. **Stop sinning or something worse may happen to you.'**

- Matthew 12:43-45 NIV:
  43 When an impure spirit comes out of a person, it goes through arid places seeking rest and does not find it.
  44 Then it says, 'I will return to the house I left.' When it arrives, it finds the house unoccupied, swept clean and put in order.
  45 Then it goes and takes with it seven other spirits more wicked than itself, and they go in and live there. **And the final condition of that person is worse than the first.** That is how it will be with this wicked generation.

- 2 Peter 2:20-21 NIV:
  20 If they have escaped the corruption of the world by knowing our Lord and Savior Jesus Christ and are again entangled in it and are overcome, **they are worse off at the end** than they were at the beginning.

21 It would have been **better for them not to have known** the way of right-eousness, than to have known it and then to turn their backs on the sacred command that was passed on to them.

So how do we prevent evil spirits from returning to their former victims? By assisting each delivered victim to identify, renounce, repent of, and stop the poor thinking, bad decision-making, unwise choice of friends, sinful habits, generation curses, and ungodly vows that individually and collectively are the open doors which allowed the demons to oppress or possess them in the first place.

Not only this, but simply repenting alone by itself is not enough. In addition, new thoughts and new habits and new ways learned from God's Word must be put in their place. All of this can take time (weeks, months and even years if not undertaken with vigor), while meanwhile the former victim's defenses against the evil one is weakened.

This subject of how to achieve successful lasting demonic deliverance could rightly be an entire separate book and class all by itself. So given this short class format, the best advice we can give you is this: cast out demons wherever and whenever you find them without hesitation, just as Jesus instructed us to do, but then promptly seek help from others as described next.

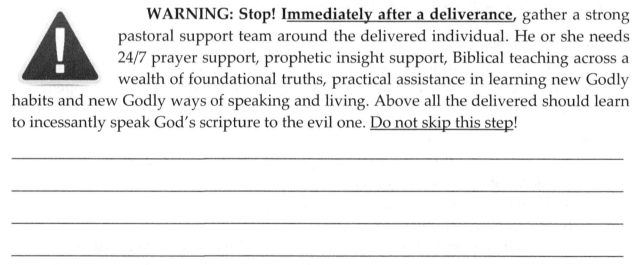

WARNING: Stop! <u>Immediately after a deliverance,</u> gather a strong pastoral support team around the delivered individual. He or she needs 24/7 prayer support, prophetic insight support, Biblical teaching across a wealth of foundational truths, practical assistance in learning new Godly habits and new Godly ways of speaking and living. Above all the delivered should learn to incessantly speak God's scripture to the evil one. <u>Do not skip this step</u>!

_____

_____

_____

_____

4.3.7 Illustrative Testimonies: Casting Out Demons

 <u>For the full video recorded testimony, see page 5.</u>

Testimony 1: Class instructor Paul's mother made an ill-fated attempt to cast out a demon, while a good prophetic friend of Paul's in our local area taught a demonic deliverance class that on its very first class attempt to cast out a demon ended in disaster.

Key takeaway lesson: how <u>not</u> to attempt to cast out demons!

Testimony 2: The author's father was a career U.S. Air Force captain who after his retirement from service worked for nearly three decades in various military VA Hospitals. During the course of caring for 5,000 mentally ill patients of all types over a period of 27 years, the author's father conducted experiments on thousands of them using John 3:16 in the Bible. The author's father was able to decisively demonstrate to Veteran's Administration officials that fully one-half (50%) of all medically diagnosed mental ill patients were actually not mentally ill at all, but rather were forcibly possessed against their will by demons (incredible!). The author's father was consistently able cast these demons out, resulting in what seemed to be their immediate "healing."

Key takeaway lesson: learn how to use God's Word as a "spiritual diagnostic tool" of sorts… while always seeking the prophetic guidance of the Holy Spirit in everything we do, which always must replace our plans.

Testimony 3: Casting a demon out of a man in a local Christian church.

Key takeaway lesson: learn how the renunciation of bad beliefs and repentance of sin are not the same things; <u>both</u> are necessary component keys to lasting demonic deliverance, or the problem will return in time.

Testimony 4: Casting a demon out of a woman on the front row of a local area Christian church in a disguised manner, to avoid causing an unnecessary disturbance or worse in that unprepared church. The root cause was her self-admitted habit of saying, "I can't understand (the parables and teachings of Jesus)" combined with her expressing her viewpoint that "Psalms is so simple to understand compared to (the Gospel books)." In time this led to evil spirits gaining the "legal right" to make her words her reality.

Key takeaway lesson: learn why it can be an act of wisdom in some cases to *not* tell a victim that evil spirit is the cause of his or her problems, and instead simply just take action.

Testimony 5: Story of a woman who successfully went through a partial deliverance, only to come under attack on her way home.

Key takeaway lesson: Learn how to preempt evil spirits before they can strike those who need deliverance (*something we constantly do now!*).

<u>Testimony 6</u>: Story of a neighbor friend who unwittingly opened the door for a paralyzing demonic attack of fear on herself as a direct result of her well-intended, but incorrectly worded prayers for her husband and children.

Key takeaway lesson: understand the tremendous power our words have, even in our private prayers to God; learn how to pray correctly for our children so we are blessing them rather than inadvertently cursing them!

Additional Class Notes (Lesson Four)

Your Personal Notes, Observations, and Class Activities

_____

_____

_____

_____

_____

_____

_____

_____

_____

_____

_____

_____

_____

_____

_____

_____

_____

_____

_____

_____

Questions for the Instructors or the class:

1. _____

_____

_____

_____

_____

2. _____

_____

_____

_____

_____

3. _____

_____

_____

_____

_____

4.4 Walking It Out – Class Assignment (LESSON FOUR)

WALKING IT OUT Class Assignment (Lesson Four)

OUR ACTION PLAN

Seek **JESUS** at a *level and depth that you may not have previously* to continually further develop and deepen your intimate, personal relationship with Jesus.

Continued Class Action Assignments

Read Daily: "Expect to Believe: 90 Bible Devotionals to Increase Your Faith for the Impossible" by Paul Williams (expect a close encounter with the Holy Spirit to happen while reading these devotionals daily).

Watch / Listen to the Class Lesson Videos; pause when needed to read-pray scriptures, work Action Plan steps, work Homework Challenges and Go Deeper **as** you go through your class notes AGAIN. (*Journaling revelations Holy Spirit has shown you*)

Review Weekly: Key Learning Objectives (*check off each one as you achieve the objectives of this week's lesson (see this chapter's Introduction). Ask the Holy Spirit to plant these objectives deep in your heart and mind and help put them into practice in your daily life.*

Suggested Action: fast, creating an intimate relationship with God: (*per section 1.2 apply the three key takeaways that the author learned*). God responds to fasting and prayer. *Adding a Biblically based food-fast is even better and can aid in combination with God's Word and prayer to a significant breakthrough (see section 1.12) Speak aloud* **the action items in the seven steps taken from James 4:7-10** (*especially steps 5& 6 (see section 1.12)*).

Daily abide in the overflow of the anointing of Holy Spirit (*as described in sections 1.5 and 1.6*). Ask the Holy Spirit **every day** to **soften your heart and fill you with God's amazing love** for Your fellow created human beings. Re-commit to earnestly seeking the Holy Ghost in His fullness in your life.

Daily read and apply the books of _John, Acts, and Ephesians_[14] *(see section 1.12)* using the "read-pray the Word approach and the seven steps to "Intimate Relationship with God."

Assignments for Lesson Four →

Re-review the action steps in Chapters One, Two, and Three to make sure you practice them in your daily walk with God.

Review, Learn, Understand: (the main learning objectives for this Chapter 4).

Read aloud all scriptures in section 4.2.

Know without any doubt there is absolute power in HIS *(Jesus)* Name, as given HIM by the Father, as you read *Philippians 2:9-11 and James 2:19.*

Read and meditate on: *Power of God's Word in our life in general scriptures.* Hebrews 4:12, John 15:7, John 6:63 *(see section 4.3.3).*

Re-study Jesus' ministry: (see section 4.3.3).

Read again the scriptures regarding demons causing disease and mental illness: (see section 4.3.4).

HOMEWORK CHALLENGE

1. The source of our power is the _____.

2. Why should we not use formulaic thinking in our prayers?

_____

_____

_____

_____

---

[14] In our observation, no other combination of three books in the Bible gives as much spiritual return for the time expended. These three books serve as an effective jumping point to real-pray the remainder of the entire Bible.

3. Why did Jesus heal four separate cases of the same physical condition in four completely different ways?

_____

_____

_____

4. What is the key you learned in John 14:26?

_____

_____

5. The more we pray _____, the more frequently and clearly we hear the voice of the Holy Spirit, which ultimately leads to us doing the works that Jesus did as He told us we would in John 14:12-13.

6. How does 1 Corinthians chapter 12 apply the concept of the body's many diverse parts to the body of Christ (the church) healing the sick?

_____

_____

_____

7. Why does it not work to pray asking God to "make Satan obey me"? Instead, what should we do? Use _____ to force Satan to acknowledge our authority over him.

8. Why could Satan not keep the house in the skit by your class instructors?

_____

_____

_____

9. Why did Satan lose his battle with Jesus?

_____

_____

10. God's Word decides every battle in the _____ and in the supernatural for both sides.

11. If you rebuke physical symptom in the name of Jesus when a person is sick or injured because of bodily oppression or possession, will this result in their healing?

_____

_____

12. Why is it a better approach to use wisdom when demons are present and a physical healing is desired? (See section 4.3.4).

_____

_____

_____

13. What are two clues that Jesus gave us for what should be done to prevent physical healings or the return of evil spirits found to their victims as found in John 5:14 and Matthew 12:45)?

_____

_____

14. _____ insight from the Holy Spirit is extremely powerful and must always replace any approach of our own when casting out demons.

15. Jesus not only delegated His authority over demons to us, but He also _____ us to cast out demons in Matthew 10:1,9.

16. Based on section 4.3.6, list the open doors which allow demonic oppression or possession to occur.

_____

_____

_____

17. Why is simple repentance alone not enough to close some demonic entry points?

_____

_____

_____

_____

18. What post-deliverance support ministry support is immediately needed for a person who has just been delivered from demons? (_preferably such support is already operating and available in your church or a full-gospel church in your area_)

_____

_____

_____

_____

19. When we come under attack by our enemy and hear lies, we should immediately REBUKE the enemy and replace those thoughts with what?

_____

_____

_____

_____

GOING DEEPER (Journal Time)

1. Why did Jesus heal four different blind men in four completely different ways? What does this show you about physical healings?

_____

_____

2. What did you learn from the "stolen house" skit?

_____

_____

3. Why did the evil spirits say, "Jesus I know, and Paul I know about, but who are you" (Acts 19:13-16)?

_____

_____

4. Why does the author recommend soliciting the assistance of experienced pastors or leaders who already have an established ministry for a person needing post-deliverance help?_____

_____

_____

Does your church or a church or ministry in your area offer post-deliverance ministry support? _____
_____. If your church does not, then consider asking why not.

There is no time like the present to begin preparing yourself for demonic deliverance because this support can immensely help the Jesus' church to walk in freedom.

5

Handling Problematic Situations

OBJECTIVES OF LESSON 5:

- Understand the differences between healing Christians and non-Christians.
- Understand how Christians can keep their healing.
- Understand Paul's 'Thorn in the Flesh.'
- Review limitations to use of our authority in Christ.
- Staying pure to be a special vessel for God's use.

5.1 Healing Christians versus Non-Christians

We originally began discussing this subject in Chapter 2, but now it is time to dive much deeper. It is important to thoroughly understand the significant differences in thinking and tactics between healing Christians versus non-believers, as well as the issue of what's needed to keep Christians healed. Let us start with scripture:

- Mathew 25:14-18, 28-30 NIV (Jesus' parable of the talents):
  14 Again, it will be like a man going on a journey, who called his servants and entrusted his wealth to them.
  15 To one he gave five bags of gold, to another two bags, and to another one bag, each according to his ability. Then he went on his journey.
  16 **The man who had received five bags of gold went at once and put his money to work and gained five bags more.**
  17 **So also, the one with two bags of gold gained two more.**
  18 But the man who had received one bag went off, dug a hole in the ground and hid his master's money.
  [...]

28 'So take the bag of gold from (the man who failed to invest his 1 talent) and give it to the one who has ten bags.
29 For whoever has will be given more, and they will have an abundance. Whoever does not have, even what they have will be taken from them.
30 And throw that worthless servant outside, into the darkness, where there will be weeping and gnashing of teeth.'

Comment: never has the saying, *"Use It Or Lose It"* been more applicable!

- Luke 12:47 NIV: The servant who knows the master's will and does not get ready or does not do what the master wants will be beaten with many blows. 48 But the one who does not know and does things deserving punishment will be beaten with few blows. **From everyone who has been given much, much will be demanded; and from the one who has been entrusted with much, much more will be asked.**

- Matthew 7:1-2 NIV (Jesus): Do not judge, or you too will be judged. **For in the same way, you judge others, you will be judged**, and with the measure you use, it will be measured to you.

Comment: As Christians, after years of hearing countless unclear or conflicting sermons and messages in churches and online, unfortunately our understanding can become mixed with varying amounts of erroneous thinking and bad doctrine, along with a generous scoop of unbelief. Because the average Christian in the western world does not intensively study God's Word for themselves, such believers are often unable to accurately distinguish between what is right and wrong.

Their mixed beliefs, combined with the silent erosion of faith caused by hundreds of unanswered prayers over the years due to their poor understanding of how God's promises work, combines to diminish their faith until precious little of it remains for even receiving their own physical healing, never mind for healing others.

Even worse yet, since many mature, well-established Christians refuse to use what little bit of faith they may have left, this puts them at the very real risk of losing even their last little bit of faith (see Mathew 25:29 quoted above).

Meanwhile, the divine principle that *"from everyone who has been given much, much will be demanded"* raises the bar of faith so that the miraculous becomes difficult for them to even *understand*, never mind personally *experience*, never mind actually *do*.

Finally, for those Christians who teach others the faith bar is even higher yet:

- James 3:1 NIV: Not many of you should become teachers, my fellow believers, because you know that **we who teach will be judged more strictly.**

We as Christians are judged by God by our years of teaching Biblical truths to our own children and witnessing to non-believers. We teach our children that the Bible is true and that through Jesus' resurrection victory over our enemy that He has all power in heaven and in earth and that Jesus saves, delivers, and heals.

_____

_____

_____

_____

5.1.1 Impact of Bad Doctrine, Fear, & Unforgiveness

Sadly, through lack of knowledge and fear, well-established Christians have very often failed to act on the words of Jesus to do the things He did. Because of the divine principal "to him much is given, much is required" and that "teachers are judged more strictly," this means healing our fellow Christians can be far more challenging than is healing unbelievers.

Specifically, two problems more all others often undermine whatever faith and knowledge mature Christians may have left for the miraculous:

- The ill-advised words –and plain dead wrong words-- that many mature Christians incessantly speak, and;

- Unforgiveness and even bitterness for relatives, church members, themselves, pastors, and even God Himself.

How can we help these Christians to receive their physical healing? A dramatic case history example is coming up which we will use as a learning aid in order to fully understand exactly what is wrong and how to correct it.

_____

_____

_____

_____

5.2 How to Help Christians Keep Their Healing

Not only can it be a challenge to help Christians receive their healing in the first place, but it can be even harder yet for them to *keep* their healing once it occurs.

The reality is that as hard as it can be to heal mature Christians in the first place, they often lose their healing in less than a day – and sometimes in a matter of mere *minutes* – after being healed by Jesus. Your class instructors have personally witnessed many dramatic cases of this. In one example a mature Christian was instantly and completely healed on the spot of an extremely painful, chronic limb joint failure condition which needed surgical replacement, only to hours later that same day lose all trace of the healing in just a matter of minutes after failing to speak up and publicly give glory to Jesus when the opportunity presented itself.

The massive culprit in all such lost healing cases is the same: the doubting words that come from our lips, and/or the failure to speak words of faith. We must understand how to instruct our mature Christians believers they can be healed in the first place, then continue to keep their healing. Note: several dramatic healing cases which illustrate this point will be discussed over the remainder of this class.

_____

_____

_____

_____

5.3 Illustrative Testimony: Chronic Heart Failure

 <u>For the full video recorded testimony, see page 5</u>.

<u>For the full video recorded testimony, see page 5</u>.

<u>Testimony</u> from April 2022 of a man with congestive heart failure wearing a life vest to keep him alive who was facing near-hopeless odds of surviving heart surgery.

Key takeaways: how to help mature Christians forsake their bad doctrines and poor thinking about God and His healing power while sharply raising their faith in Jesus so they can receive their physical healing… and keep it.

Finally, here is the biggest takeaway lesson for all of us: let's all make sure that what we speak with our lips aligns closely with the Word of God, or don't speak at all! (re-review as necessary Chapters 1 and 3).

5.4 Understanding Paul's 'Thorn in the Flesh'

Caution: in the experience of your class instructors, it is both unnecessary –as well as often unwise—to attempt to tackle the issue head on of what is known as "Paul's thorn in the flesh" (more on this next) before healing a mature Christian who has raised this issue. Instead, it is wise to sidestep this issue until *after* they have been healed when their heart is soft and open.

How? This can be done by sidestepping this objection and instead simply magnifying Jesus. In the rare case that magnifying Jesus does not work on a subject, then nothing you could have said or done would have worked anyway – each objection you answered would only have led to yet another.

So, what is "Paul's thorn in the flesh"? Let us read what the Apostle Paul wrote:

- 2 Corinthians 12:6 NIV:
  6 Even if I should choose to boast, I would not be a fool, because I would be speaking the truth. But I refrain, so no one will think more of me than is warranted by what I do or say,
  7 or because of these surpassingly great revelations. Therefore, in order to keep me from becoming conceited, **I was given a thorn in my flesh, a messenger of Satan, to torment me.**
  8 Three times I pleaded with the Lord to take it away from me.
  9 **But he said to me, 'My grace is sufficient for you, for my power is made perfect in weakness.'** Therefore, I will boast all the more gladly about my weaknesses, so that Christ's power may rest on me.
  10 That is why, for Christ's sake, I delight in weaknesses, in insults, in hardships, in persecutions, in difficulties. For when I am weak, then I am strong.

Many mature Christians are quick to quote this scripture to explain their lack of faith for their own healing and in particular to justify their refusal to pray for the healing of others. It's amazing how in a church of 500 people these objectors seem to think that all 500 people in attendance have Paul's "thorn in the flesh." So they will not pray for any of them to be healed, despite Jesus' command to do so.

As believers in divine healing, we must have an answer on this point for those who are open to receiving it (be aware that some are not, no matter what is said or done).

To do so effectively, let's take a step back first. First of all, we know that "all Scripture is God-breathed" (2 Timothy 3:16 NIV), and it is logical that we can *count* on God's truth to never contradict itself.

However, at first glance, scripture may *seem* to contradict itself in certain places.

So how do we resolve such apparent conflicts? We can do so by reviewing the *totality* of scriptures on a given point of confusion. By doing so, an understanding can be readily discerned which agrees with God's character, nature, promises and the totality of the Bible, all at the same time.

_____

_____

_____

_____

So let us do this now with "Paul's thorn in the flesh."

First, we know from seven difference passages in Matthew, Mark, Luke, John, and Acts that *everyone* who came to Jesus and His disciples were healed, no matter what disease or illness they had[15]. Here are three examples of these seven scriptures (all seven will appear later in this book):

- Luke 4:40 NLT:
  "As the sun went down that evening, people throughout the village brought sick family members to Jesus. **No matter what their diseases were, the touch of his hand healed every one.**"

- Matthew 10:1 NIV:
  Jesus called his twelve disciples to him and gave them authority to drive out impure spirits and **to heal every disease and sickness**.

_____

[15] These seven scriptures will be examined in detail in Lesson 10, *"Satan's 10 Blocks to Healing."*

- Acts 5:16 NIV (the disciples):
  Crowds gathered also from the towns around Jerusalem, bringing their sick and those tormented by impure spirits, and **all of them were healed**.

Furthermore, we know that through Jesus' sacrifice of the cross He won complete victory for us of all of our sins and all of our sicknesses alike:

- 1 Peter 2:24 NLT:
  24 "He personally carried our sins
  in his body on the cross
  so that we can be dead to sin
  and live for what is right.
  By his wounds
  you are healed."

This scripture does not say, "most but not all of your sins are forgiven" or "most but not all of your diseases are healed" or "everyone is healed except Paul and his thorn in the flesh," etc. If so, then Jesus' victory on the cross was not total and complete.

Therefore, we can logically conclude that Paul's thorn in the flesh simply *could not have been* disease or illness, since to believe this would mar the totality of Jesus' once-and-for-all victory for all humanity, past, present, and future.

This concept is fully backed up in Psalms:

Psalms 103:2, 3 NIV:
Praise the Lord, my soul,
and forget not all his benefits—
3 who forgives **all** your sins
and heals **all** your diseases.

So given these scriptures we can logically conclude that Paul's "thorn" may have been something personal and unpleasant that Paul simply did not like about himself and just wanted gone for his own personal reasons… which would also explain why he did not state what the bothersome problem was.

Possible examples of this type of personal problem could have been a birthmark or wart on Paul's face, a balding head, an odd way of walking, or even Paul's, timid or hesitant manner of speaking on some occasions. Actually, there is good evidence for the latter in the following scripture passages written by Paul about himself:

- 1 Corinthians 2:1-5 NIV:

  2 And so it was with me, brothers and sisters. When I came to you, **I did not come with eloquence or human wisdom** as I proclaimed to you the testimony about God.

  2 For I resolved to know nothing while I was with you except Jesus Christ and him crucified.

  3 I came to you in weakness with great fear and trembling.

  4 My message and my preaching **were not with wise and persuasive words**, but with a demonstration of the Spirit's power,

  5 so that your faith might not rest on human wisdom, but on God's power.

- 2 Corinthians 10:10 NLT:

  For some say, "Paul's letters are demanding and forceful, **but in person he is weak, and his speeches are worthless!**"

Because these scripture passages somewhat match Paul's previous description of his thorn in the flesh and its humbling effect on him, then perhaps Paul's thorn in the flesh was an embarrassing occasional problem with "stage fright." If so, of course God used this this problem to teach Paul to rely on the power of the Holy Spirit to more than make up the difference.

Nevertheless, whatever Paul's thorn in the flesh may have been 2,000 years ago, it has no bearing whatsoever on Jesus' command to us today to go teach, preach, cast out demons, and heal people of every tribe and nation on earth to pave the way for His second coming to earth.

5.5 Limitations to Use of Our Authority

Jesus made no effort to heal everyone in the land of Israel all at once with a single command. Nor did He wave His hand to heal everyone all at once in a village that fervently believed in him, or even heal everyone at once in the crowds that followed Him everywhere He went.

Instead, Jesus healed the sick one person at a time as they individually so choose to come and seek Him in faith, one-by-one.

Building forward on Jesus' example, then this means His apostles Peter and Paul truly did greater miracles than Jesus did, just as Jesus said His disciples would do in John 14:12. Peter's shadow healed people in mass, while Paul's handkerchiefs healed those who touched them. However, even then Peter and Paul still only healed those who came seeking help by faith.

This leads us to several important observations about the practical limits of our authority in Christ to cast out demons and to heal the sick and injured today:

- We can only heal those who are open to and seeking our assistance – either because they directly asked us for our help, or because the Holy Spirit sovereignly points them out to us.

- We cannot heal people who are unrelated to us without their request or permission.

- We *can* pray for our **minor** children to be delivered or healed <u>without</u> their agreement, or even sometimes as may be necessary <u>without</u> their knowledge as well! Caution: never attempt to dodge the bold exercise of your faith, as God knows your motives and will not honor a deliberate lack of faith.

- We must have the consent of our **grown** children in order to fully heal them or fully deliver them from demonic influence.

- We *can* exercise a limited amount of authority over our close relatives whether they give us permission or not -- or even whether they know it or not! Additionally, we can exercise our authority whether they are in our direct presence or in states or countries far away.

 <u>For the full video recorded testimony, see page 5</u>.

<u>Illustrative testimony of this point</u>: a brief case history.

- Finally, we can likewise exercise a certain amount of restraining authority over *anyone* who is in our home or property, or *anyone* who is in our presence, almost no matter where we are (on our property, in public, or even on *their* property). For example, we can speak to a robber's gun who is pointing it at you and command it to misfire.

_____

_____

_____

_____

Here are some practical ministry points to remember:

- Always work directly in person hands-on with those in need whenever possible and practical. There are numerous powerful and lasting direct and secondary benefits to loving the sick and injured in their homes wherever and whenever possible!

- Healing by video conference session, telephone call, chat messages and even cell phone text messages (!) all work also, listed here in order of the least communication difficulty and greatest success rate.

- Working through third party relatives or friends of the sick should be our very last resort, for multiple reasons – starting very importantly with getting and keeping the subject healed.

For the full video recorded testimony, see page 5.

Illustrative testimony of this point: (*short testimony of how to be successful in such cases*).

_____

_____

_____

_____

Reminder once again: follow the lead of the Holy Spirit! For those who have spent the necessary time to develop and confirm your ability to hear the guidance of the Holy Spirit and match it to God's Word and His revealed character and nature, the Holy Spirit's directions should always displace every plan and course of action of our own that we may have formulated, no matter how experienced and sound our plan may seem.

_____

_____

_____

_____

5.6 Staying Pure for God's Special Use

Before we begin, let us be clear that the issue at stake here **is not** salvation! With this in mind, let us carefully example God's Word on the issue of striving for Biblical purity.

First, notice the deliberate use of the word *purity* in the last sentence. We should never attempt to work toward our "righteousness," since our right-standing before God is only possible because of the blood of Jesus sacrificed on our behalf – absolutely nothing we can ever do could ever justify us before our Father God.

Second, Jesus does not condemn (John 8:1-11). Rather, He draws us *away* from our sins through His amazing love. For this reason, scriptural passages about purity should be taken as Godly *exhortation* rather than demonic *condemnation*.

Now we will examine just four of 42 different scripture passages in the New Testament of the Bible on the twin subjects of obedience and purity:

- 2 Timothy 2:20-24 NLT:
  20 "In a wealthy home some utensils are made of gold and silver, and some are made of wood and clay. The expensive utensils are used for special occasions, and the cheap ones are for everyday use.
  21 **If you keep yourself pure, you will be a special utensil for honorable use. Your life will be clean, and you will be ready for the Master to use you for every good work.**
  22 **Run** from anything that stimulates youthful lusts {*your class instructors: never mind the actual sin of lust itself!*}. **Instead,** pursue righteous living, faithfulness, love, and peace. Enjoy the companionship of those who call on the Lord with pure hearts.
  23 Again I say, don't get involved in foolish, ignorant arguments that only start fights.
  24 A servant of the Lord must not quarrel but must be kind to everyone, be able to teach, and be patient with difficult people."

- Luke 11:36 NLT:

  If you are filled with light, **with no dark corners**, then your whole life will be radiant, as though a floodlight were filling you with light.

- 1 John 3:2-10 NLT:

  2 Dear friends, we are already God's children, but he has not yet shown us what we will be like when Christ appears. But we do know that we will be like him, for we will see him as he really is.

  3 And all who have this eager expectation **will keep themselves pure, just as he is pure.**

  4 Everyone who sins are breaking God's law, for all sin is contrary to the law of God.

  5 And you know that Jesus came to take away our sins, and there is no sin in him.

  6 **Anyone who continues to live in him will not sin. But anyone who keeps on sinning does not know him or understand who he is.**

  7 Dear children, don't let anyone deceive you about this: When people do what is right, it shows that they are righteous, even as Christ is righteous. 8 But when people keep on sinning, it shows that they belong to the devil, who has been sinning since the beginning. But the Son of God came to destroy the works of the devil.

  9 Those who have been born into God's family **do not make a practice of sinning,** because God's life is in them. So they can't keep on sinning, because they are children of God.

  10 So now we can tell who are children of God and who are children of the devil. Anyone who does not live righteously and does not love other believers does not belong to God.

- 1 John 3:21-22 NLT:

  21 Dear friends, **if we don't feel guilty,** we can come to God with bold confidence.

  22 **And we will receive from him whatever we ask because we obey him and do the things that please him.**

5.7 Class Subsection

How can we increase our faith? The answer is given in the Bible:

- Romans 10:17 NIV:
  "Consequently, faith comes from hearing the message, and the message is heard through **the word about Christ**."

Notice that faith does not come by *praying* for more faith—after all, it takes faith to pray for faith—but rather, faith comes by *hearing* the Word about Christ.

"Hearing" the Word about Christ? Isn't "reading" the same thing? Fellow believers, let us not read scripture and then "interpret it" into what it is "supposed to mean."

Instead, let us learn to take it at face value. Do not add anything to it. Simply ask, "What does the Bible say?"

Silently reading the Word of God to ourselves is what we must do when we have no other alternative. But *speaking* the Word of God out loud to ourselves can be more effective. Why?

When we speak the Word of God out loud, more of our brain becomes involved: first, to optically recognize and understand the words; second, to audibly pronounce the words; and a third time, when our brain's auditory circuits hear the spoken Word and process it yet again. This amplification process allows more opportunity for the Holy Spirit to work on our minds and increase our understanding and retention of the Bible.

In this note, then, here are the words of Christ, which you can read aloud to yourself today:

- John 14:12-14 NIV: [Jesus said]:
  "Very truly I tell you, whoever believes in me will do the works I have been doing, and they will do even greater things than these, because I am going to the Father. And I will do whatever you ask in my name, so that the Father may be glorified in the Son. You may ask me for anything in my name, and I will do it."

Repeatedly speak the above scripture passage aloud to yourself until you know it by heart and it becomes a part of you.

Let's commit once again to daily immerse ourselves in and be inspired and changed by the living words of our Lord and Savior Jesus. Be blessed this week in Jesus' mighty name!

_____

_____

_____

_____

Additional Class Notes (Lesson Five)

Your Personal Notes, Observations, and Class Activities

_____

_____

_____

_____

_____

_____

_____

_____

_____

_____

_____

_____

_____

_____

_____

_____

_____

_____

_____

_____

_____

_____

Questions for the Instructors or the class:

1. _____

_____

_____

_____

_____

2. _____

_____

_____

_____

_____

3. _____

_____

_____

_____

_____

5.8 Walking It Out – Class Assignment (LESSON FIVE)

WALKING IT OUT Class Assignment (LESSON FIVE)

<u>OUR ACTION PLAN</u>

<u>*Seek* **JESUS** at a *level and depth that you may not have previously* to continually further develop and deepen your intimate, personal relationship with Jesus.</u>

Continued Class Action Assignments

Read Daily: "Expect to Believe: 90 Bible Devotionals to Increase Your Faith for the Impossible" by Paul Williams (expect a close encounter with the Holy Spirit to happen while reading these devotionals daily).

Watch / Listen to the Class Lesson Videos; pause when needed to read-pray scriptures, work Action Plan steps, work Homework Challenges and Go Deeper **as** you go through your class notes AGAIN. (*Journaling revelations Holy Spirit has shown you*)

Review Weekly: Key Learning Objectives (*check off each one as you achieve the objectives of this week's lesson (see this chapter's Introduction). Ask the Holy Spirit to plant these objectives deep in your heart and mind and help put them into practice in your daily life.*

Suggested Action: fast, creating an intimate relationship with God: (*per section 1.2 apply the three key takeaways that Paul learned*) God responds to fasting and prayer. <u>*Adding a Biblically based food-fast is even better and can aid in combination with God's Word and prayer to a significant breakthrough*</u> (*per section 1.12*) <u>**Speak aloud** the action items in the seven steps taken from **James 4:7-10**</u> (*especially steps 5& 6 (see section 1.12)*)

Daily abide in the overflow of the anointing of Holy Spirit (*as described in sections 1.5 and 1.6*). Ask the Holy Spirit **every day** to **soften your heart and fill you with God's amazing love** for Your fellow created human beings. Re-commit to earnestly seeking the Holy Ghost in His fullness in your life.

Daily read and apply the books of _John, Acts, and Ephesians_[16] *(see section 1.12)* using the "read-pray the Word approach" and the "Seven Steps to Intimate Relationship with God."

Ask the Holy Spirit to guard your mouth and direct your path. Focus on speaking what the Holy Spirit leads you to say, going where the Holy Spirit directs you to go, and doing what the Holy Spirit says to do.

Action Assignments for Lesson Five →

Read Hebrews chapter 11 the "great faith chapter" in its entirety.

Teach our children that the Bible is true. *(see section 5.1)*

Develop a thorough understanding of the differences between healing Christians versus non-believers, and what keeps them healed. *(see sections 5.1, 5.2)*

Study the scriptures concerning "Paul's thorn in the flesh." Make note of the caution given concerning the healing of mature Christians.

Learn and commit to memory the practical limits of our authority in Christ to cast out demons and to heal the sick and injured. *(see section 5.5)*

Always follow the lead of the Holy Spirit! His directions must always immediately displace every plan and course of action of our own.

Silently reading the Word of God to ourselves is what we must do when we have no other alternative. But speaking the Word of God out loud to ourselves can be more effective *(see section 5.7)*.

Read and pray over the final sub-section of today's lesson[17]:

---

[16] In our observation, no other combination of three books in the Bible gives as much spiritual return for the time expended. These three books serve as an effective jumping point to read

-pray the remainder of the entire Bible.

[17] This material was excepted from Chapter 37, "How to Increase Your Faith (still more)" of the book "Expect to Believe: 90 Devotionals to Increase Your Faith for the Impossible."

HOMEWORK CHALLENGE

1. What happens when Christians do not study God's Word for themselves?

_____

_____

_____

2. What key Biblical truths should we be quick to instruct our children and new believers in?

_____

_____

_____

_____

3. Why does the faith of long-time Christians tend to diminish and the miraculous becomes difficult to comprehend?

_____

_____

_____

_____

4. Is the faith bar higher for teachers of the Word? _____

Why?_____

_____

_____

5. What two factors undermine the faith and knowledge mature Christians may have about the miraculous?

_____

_____

_____

_____

6. What are the top two huge culprits behind why some Christians lose their healing?

_____

_____

_____

_____

_____

GOING DEEPER (Journal Time)

1. As a Christian believing that God heals, what is your take on "Paul's thorn in the flesh"? Will such objections hinder your prayers for a believer who wants to be healed?

_____

_____

2. We have read and pondered over some practical ministry points to remember. What are they?

_____

_____

3. Which is ranked number one and why? Which would you prefer and why?

_____

_____

4. Are you listening for the Holy Spirit to speak? Do you journal on a daily basis concerning the Holy Spirit's directions?

_____

_____

5. Have you been impacted by bad doctrine? How has this affected you?

_____

_____

6

Gifts of the Holy Spirit, Part 1 of 2

HERE ARE OUR LEARNING objectives for Lesson 6:

- Christian humor: Understanding the most important factor to miracle working.
- Understand the nine (9) Fruits of The Holy Spirit.
- Understand the nine (9) Gifts of The Holy Spirit.

6.1 What Is Most Important to Miracle Working?

We will begin this lesson with a lighthearted class poll. Considering everything we have learned in our class lessons so far, what is the single most important factor to work a miracle?

Your five voting choices are:

1) The mighty name of Jesus?
2) The power and fire of the Holy Spirit?
3) God's Word the Bible?
4) Our faith in God and His promises?
5) Using our authority by speaking with our lips?

Answer: (your class instructors will provide the correct answer in our in-person classes and via our free online video instruction – see page 5).

Here is a convenient summary of the complete answer:

"When we believers speak God's Word boldly with our lips in the name of Jesus through the Holy Spirit's power indwelling within us, the result is signs, wonders, and miracles for the glory of God."

Where can we find this in the Bible? All five elements appear in the following powerful scripture passage which brings everything together in one place:

- Acts 4:29-31 NIV (Peter, John and the Apostles in prayer to God):
  29 "Now, Lord (...) enable your servants to **speak** your **word** with great **boldness**.
  30 Stretch out your hand to heal and perform signs and wonders through the name of your holy servant **Jesus**."
  31 After they prayed, the place where they were meeting was shaken. And they were all **filled with the Holy Spirit** and spoke the word of God boldly.

Important: speaking *forcefully* and/or *loudly* is neither important nor helpful in working a miracle, although speaking *boldly* <u>always</u> is (whether in a loud or quiet voice). This is because speaking *forcefully* typically is a manifestation of our *emotions*, whereas speaking with *boldness* is a manifestation our *faith*.

_____

_____

_____

_____

6.2 The Nine <u>Fruits</u> of the Holy Spirit

One of the very first manifestations of Jesus and the Holy Spirit dwelling within us is the softening of our hearts with genuine love, consideration, kindness, and the other traits of God's divine nature.

The Holy Spirit will birth and <u>grow</u> His nine (9) *fruits* of the character and nature of Jesus in the lives of every Christian individually as He is so allowed to do so:

- Galatians 5:22-23 NLT:
  22 But the Holy Spirit produces this kind of fruit in our lives: **love, joy, peace, patience, kindness, goodness, faithfulness,**
  23 **gentleness, and self-control.** There is no law against these things!

- 2 Peter 1:5-6 NIV:

  5 For this very reason, make every effort to add to your faith goodness; and to goodness, knowledge;

  6 and to knowledge, self-control; and to self-control, perseverance; and to perseverance, godliness;

  7 and to godliness, mutual affection; and to mutual affection, love.

  8 **For if you possess these qualities in increasing measure,** they will keep you from being ineffective and unproductive in your knowledge of our Lord Jesus Christ.

_____

_____

_____

_____

6.3 The Nine <u>Gifts</u> of The Holy Spirit (Introduction)

In addition to the nine (9) *fruits* of the Holy Spirit listed in the previous sub-section, for those believers who actively seek Him the Holy Spirit has nine (9) *gifts* which He sovereignly gives to us as He so sees fit.

Note: This short 10-week Bible Study class series is not intended to be a replacement for a 2-year or 4-year Holy Spirit-based Bible College program.

Instead, this short class series is only a brief *introduction* to the Holy Spirit and His gifts, which is sufficient with regular practice to become effective laborers on the front lines in the Kingdom of God.

For detailed information on the Holy Spirit and His nine gifts, see the 161-page book *"The Holy Spirit and His Gifts"* by Kenneth E. Hagin (1995) available from your favorite online bookstore. **Today's lesson borrows substantial inspiration from this anointed book.**

Let us begin by carefully studying the nine (9) Gifts of the Holy Spirit in God's Word:

- 1 Corinthians 12:1-11 NIV:

  1 Now about the gifts of the Spirit, brothers and sisters, **I do not want you to be uninformed.**

2 You know that when you were pagans, somehow or other you were influenced and led astray to mute idols.

3 Therefore I want you to know that no one who is speaking by the Spirit of God says, 'Jesus be cursed,' and no one can say, 'Jesus is Lord,' except by the Holy Spirit.

4 There are different kinds of gifts, but the same Spirit distributes them.

5 There are different kinds of service, but the same Lord.

6 There are different kinds of workings, but in all of them and in everyone it is the same God at work.

7 Now to each one the manifestation of the Spirit is given for the common good.

8 To one there is given through the Spirit **a message of wisdom**, to another a **message of knowledge** by means of the same Spirit,

9 to another **faith** by the same Spirit, to another **gifts of healing** by that one Spirit,

10 to another **miraculous powers**, to another **prophecy**, to another **distinguishing between spirits**, to another **speaking in different kinds of tongues**, and to still another the **interpretation of tongues**.

11 All these are the work of one and the same Spirit, and He distributes them to each one, just as He determines.

_____

_____

_____

_____

<u>6.4 Nine Gifts</u> of the Holy Spirit: Detailed Review

As we engage in a careful study the nine (9) Gifts of the Holy Spirit in this section, remember throughout to heed these recommendations by the Apostle Paul:

- 1 Corinthians 12:31 NIV:
  Now **eagerly desire the greater gifts**….

- 1 Corinthians 14:1 NIV:
  Follow the way of love and **eagerly desire gifts of the Spirit, especially prophecy.**

It may take extended seasons of prayer and fasting to ensure that we have the right motives and be correctly prepared to receive more of the gifts. In the end those who continue to earnestly seek the "greater gifts" of Holy Spirit will obtain what they ask for if they do not give up!

- Matthew 7:7-8 NLT:
  7 Keep on asking, and you **will** receive what you ask for. Keep on seeking, and you **will** find. Keep on knocking, and the door **will** be opened to you.
  8 For **everyone** who asks, receives. **Everyone** who seeks, finds. And to **everyone** who knocks, the door **will** be opened.

We will know closely examine the nine (9) Gifts of the Holy Spirit one-by-one, reviewing them in the order that your instructors believe is optimal for orderly learning.

_____

_____

_____

_____

6.4.1 The Gift of Prophecy

This is an *utterance* or *inspirational* gift which communicates the heart of God:

- 1 Corinthians 12:10 NIV: …*to another **prophecy**…*

Description: the New Testament "simple" Gift of Prophecy is spoken by the Holy Spirit through believers for the edification, exhortation, and comfort of others; the best way to think of this Gift is it being the very heart of God expressed for the recipient. For this reason, this gift can be enormously powerful and life-changing for the receiver to learn the plans and purposes of God for his or her lives through this Gift.

Example:

- 1 Corinthians 14:3 NIV: But the one who prophesies speaks to people for their **strengthening, encouraging** and **comfort**. (NLT translation: *But one who prophesies* **strengthens** *others,* **encourages** *them, and* **comforts** *them.*

- 1 Corinthians 14:24, 25 NIV:
  24 But if an unbeliever or an inquirer comes in while everyone is prophesying, **they are convicted of** sin and are **brought under judgment** by all,
  25 **as the secrets of their hearts are laid bare. So, they will fall and worship God, exclaiming, 'God is really among you!'**

- Jeremiah 23:29 NIV:
  "Is not **my word like fire**," declares the Lord, "and like a **hammer** that breaks a rock in pieces?

Given that this class is entitled in full, *"Extreme Faith for Extreme Evangelism, Physical Healing, and more,"* the convicting and even arresting role of even a single word prophecy is well-worth utilizing in our evangelism efforts.

Manifestation: Most commonly, there is no revelation of the past or future in this Gift. However, those believers who regularly operate in the separate Gifts of the Word of Knowledge and Word of Wisdom (see above) may co-mingle those Gifts with their expression of this simple Gift of Prophecy. In such cases, there will be a note of revelation.

 CAUTION 1: Notice what is *not* listed in the above scripture passage -- there is no mention of *judgement, reproof,* or *correction!* Prophecy under the New Covenant of the New Testament after the resurrection of Jesus is quite different than was prophecy under the Old Covenant of the Old Testament of the Bible.

WARNING 2: STOP! Do not attempt to guide your life by personal prophecies!!! We are to be led by God's Word, the Bible and the Holy Spirit:

- 2 Timothy 3:16 NIV:
  All Scripture is God-breathed and is useful for teaching, rebuking, correcting, and training in righteousness,

- John 10:27-28 NIV (Jesus):

  27 My sheep listen to my voice; I know them, and they follow me.

- Romans 8:14 NIV:

  For those who are led by the Spirit of God are the children of God.

Many lives have been ruined by blindly following personal prophecies given by well-meaning individuals –and false "prophets" sent by our enemy to deceive, confuse, and lead astray.

The Word and the Spirit always agree. Never accept a personal prophecy from anyone without first confirming it directly yourself with the Word of God and the Holy Spirit, in that order. Additionally, as complementary confirmation, ask one or more individuals who have confirmed gifts of prophecy to pray and let you know what the Holy Spirit tells them about you.

Important: do not tell them anything about your issue, problem, question, or situation – this eliminates a significant "group think" potential error point, plus the Holy Spirit does not need your help to speak prophetically through another believer to you.

Later in this class series we will learn much more about exactly how to accurately hear from God while avoiding being misled by the enemy or our own imaginations.

6.4.2 The Gift of the Word of Knowledge

This is the first of three revelation gifts which *reveal* something:

- 1 Corinthians 12:8 NIV: ...*to **another a message of knowledge*** *by means of the same Spirit.*

Description: the Word of Knowledge is a supernatural revelation about events which have occurred in the recent or distant past, or events which are currently occurring now.

Example:

- 1 Samuel 10:20-23 NIV:
  20 When Samuel had all Israel come forward by tribes, the tribe of Benjamin was taken by lot.
  21 Then he brought forward the tribe of Benjamin, clan by clan, and Matri's clan was taken. Finally Saul son of Kish was taken. But when they looked for him, **he was not to be found.**
  22 So they inquired further of the Lord, "Has the man come here yet?"
  And the Lord said, "Yes, he has hidden himself among the supplies."
  23 They ran and brought him out, and as he stood among the people he was a head taller than any of the others.

Manifestation: the Word of Knowledge manifests through one or more of the following methods: a still, small voice (a faint whisper), a voice in one's head, visible words written on or above someone or something or projected in the air, a vivid symbolic or literal dream, faint "daydream" type images visible in one's mind, full-blown visions while fully awake, out-of-body experiences lived on scene in person, and the interpretation of tongues.

_____

_____

_____

_____

6.4.3 The Gift of the Word of Wisdom

This is the second of three revelation gifts which *reveal* something:

- 1 Corinthians 12:8 NIV: *To one there is given through the Spirit **a message of wisdom...***

Description: the Word of Wisdom is supernatural revelation about God's plans and/or events which will occur in the imminent or distant future:

- Acts 21:10, 11 NIV:
  10 After we had been there a number of days, a prophet named Agabus came down from Judea.
  11 Coming over to us, he took Paul's belt, tied his own hands and feet with it and said, **"The Holy Spirit says, 'In this way the Jewish leaders in Jerusalem will bind the owner of this belt and will hand him over to the Gentiles.'"**

Manifestation: the Word of Wisdom manifests through the same ways as with the previously described Word of Knowledge: a still, small voice (a faint whisper), a voice in one's head, visible words written on or above someone or something or projected in the air, a vivid symbolic or literal dream, faint "daydream" type images visible in one's mind, full-blown visions while fully awake, out-of-body experiences lived on scene in person, and the interpretation of tongues.

_____

_____

_____

_____

6.4.4 The Gift of the Discernment of Spirits

This is the third of three revelation gifts which _reveal_ something:

- 1 Corinthians 12:10 NIV: …_to another_ **_distinguishing between spirits._**

Description: the gift of the Discernment of spirits is supernatural insight through our <u>five physical human senses</u> and/or our human emotions (feelings) into the realm of spirits – specifically, spirits of all three types: angelic spirits, demonic spirits, and human spirits.
  Example:

- Acts 16:16-18 NIV:

  16 Once when we were going to the place of prayer, we were met by a female slave who had a spirit by which she predicted the future. She earned a great deal of money for her owners by fortune-telling.

  17 She followed Paul and the rest of us, shouting, 'These men are servants of the Most High God, who are telling you the way to be saved.'

  18 She kept this up for many days. Finally Paul became so annoyed that he turned around **and said to the spirit**, 'In the name of Jesus Christ I command you to come out of her!' At that moment, the spirit left her.

- Revelation 1:10 NIV:

  10 On the Lord's Day I was in the Spirit, and I **heard behind me** a loud voice like a trumpet,

  11 which said: 'Write on a scroll what you see and send it to the seven churches: to Ephesus, Smyrna, Pergamum, Thyatira, Sardis, Philadelphia and Laodicea.'

  12 **I turned around to see** the voice that was speaking to me. **And when I turned I saw** seven golden lampstands,

  13 and among the lampstands was someone like a son of man, dressed in a robe reaching down to his feet and with a golden sash around his chest.

  14 The hair on his head was white like wool, as white as snow, and his eyes were like blazing fire.

  15 His feet were like bronze glowing in a furnace, and his voice was like the sound of rushing waters.

  16 In his right hand he held seven stars, and coming out of his mouth was a sharp, double-edged sword. His face was like the sun shining in all its brilliance.

  17 When I **saw him**, **I fell** at his feet as though dead. Then he placed his right hand **on me** and said: 'Do not be afraid. I am the First and the Last.'

Manifestation: The Holy Spirt gift of the Discernment of spirits always operates from birth and in real time with actual events as they happen. Confusingly enough, this includes in "real time" as lived in person in visions while experiencing past or future events that are discerned through the gifts of the Word of Knowledge and the gift of the Word of Wisdom respectively). For those who have this gift of the Discernment of spirits, it operates virtually at all times without ceasing, in fact even at night when sound asleep (those who have this gift may be jolted awake with the intensity of experiencing the emotions of others far away in real time at that moment), as well as in God-sent dreams.

The Discernment of spirits is always perceived by one or more of the human body's five <u>physical</u> senses plus the recipient's actual human feelings and emotions. Specifically, this perception is always by our physical eyes, ears, smell, feel, taste, and/or the human emotions of our minds/heart – <u>not</u> in our spirits or in our inner man, as occurs with the Word of Knowledge and Word of Wisdom.

 CAUTION: Our emotions can be exceptionally challenging for us to learn to correctly perceive; for this reason, it typically requires years of effort and prayer to correctly and consistently do so. This is because this gift in every detail utilizes <u>our own actual emotions and feelings</u> – but typically unknown to us at first, since those with this gift have no way of knowing that their feelings are coming from someone else. Once it is finally recognized that the source of our emotions and feelings is not ourselves, it typically requires a bit of time and even some trial and error to identify the source. The source of this gifting may turn out to be someone we know well, or a stranger we have never met. In either case, the source may be someone located in the same room as ourselves or alternately to our surprise in a location that is many miles, states, or countries away… and again as always with this gift, in real time.

In the next chapter of this book we will hear testimonies about this Gift[18].

6.4.5 The Gifts of Healing

This is the second of three spiritual gifts that *do* something:

- 1 Corinthians 12:9 NIV: …*to another **gift<u>s</u> of healing** by that one Spirit,*

Description: the supernatural Gift<u>s</u> of Healing (plural in the Greek) is the ability to command the sick, ailing and injured to be healed in the name of Jesus. In keeping with

---

[18] See page 5 for our free online video recorded instruction and testimonies.

its name ("Gift<u>s</u>" (plural of healing), it has often been noticed in the Biblical healing community that some believers operate much more strongly in one area of healing (such deafness) than another (such as blind eyes), while meanwhile a fellow believer may operate in a reverse manner.

Important: this gift is best thought of as not something you *have*, but rather something you *do*.

Example of the Gifts of Healing in operation:

- Acts 3:6-8 NIV:
  6 Then Peter said, 'Silver or gold I do not have, **but what I do have I give you. In the name of Jesus Christ of Nazareth, walk.'**
  7 Taking him by the right hand, he helped him up, and instantly the man's feet and ankles became strong.
  8 He jumped to his feet and began to walk. Then he went with them into the temple courts, walking and jumping, and praising God.

Manifestation: While all Christians can heal the sick, those to whom the Holy Spirit has given the Gifts of Healing operate much more frequently, consistently, and profoundly in healing the sick. For example, while every Christian can heal the sick by raising the faith of the recipient for their own healing, the Holy Spirit often sovereignly moves through those with the Gifts of Healing to perform healing miracles even on those who lack faith for their own healing or even may not have been asking for it (as demonstrated in Acts 3:6-8 above).

In the next chapter we will hear inspiring testimonies about the Gifts of Healing.

_____

_____

_____

_____

6.4.6 The Gift of Working of Miracles

This is the third of three spiritual gifts that *do* something:

- 1 Corinthians 12:10 NIV: ...*to another **miraculous powers**...*

Description: the Gift of the Working of Miracles is any supernatural intervention of God in the ordinary course of nature other than physical healing, such as the ability command physical objects in nature, human manufactured devices and machinery, the weather and more to obey our spoken commands in the name of Jesus.

Example:

- I Kings 17:3-15 NIV:
3 Elijah said to her (a widow), 'Don't be afraid. Go home and do as you have said. But first make a small loaf of bread for me from what you have and bring it to me, and then make something for yourself and your son.
14 For this is what the Lord, the God of Israel, says: "The jar of flour will not be used up and the jug of oil will not run dry until the day the Lord sends rain on the land.'"
15 She went away and did as Elijah had told her. So, there was food every day for Elijah and for the woman and her family.
16 **For the jar of flour was not used up and the jug of oil did not run dry**, in keeping with the word of the Lord spoken by Elijah.

Manifestation: While all Christians have ability in this area, those to whom the Holy Spirit has given this Gift operate much more frequently, consistently, and profoundly in working such miracles.

In the next chapter of this book we will hear testimonies about this Gift.

_____

_____

_____

_____

6.4.7 The Gift of Faith

This is the first of three spiritual gifts that *do* something:

- 1 Corinthians 12:9 NIV: *to another **faith** by the same Spirit, to another gifts of healing by that one Spirit,*

Description: the supernatural Gift of Faith is faith from God which supplements and boosts our faith when our own natural faith runs short of what is needed to perform a miracle. The supernatural Gift of Faith is often necessary for performing major healing miracles. It is also often necessary for the working of miracles involving physical objects and the weather, as well as for the raising of the dead back to life. Finally, it may also be needed to expel demons in some cases.

Example:

- Mark 4:37-41 NIV:

  37 A furious squall came up, and the waves broke over the boat, so that it was nearly swamped.

  38 Jesus was in the stern, sleeping on a cushion. The disciples woke him and said to him, "Teacher, don't you care if we drown?"

  39 **He got up, rebuked the wind, and said to the waves, 'Quiet! Be still!'** Then the wind died down and it was completely calm.

  40 He said to his disciples, 'Why are you so afraid? Do you still have no faith?'

  41 They were terrified and asked each other, 'Who is this? Even the wind and the waves obey him!'

- Mark 11:22-24 NIV (Jesus):

  22 'Have faith in God,' Jesus answered.

  23 'Truly I tell you, if anyone says to this mountain, "Go, throw yourself into the sea," and does not doubt in their heart **but believes that what they say will happen**, it will be done for them.

  24 Therefore I tell you, whatever you ask for in prayer, **believe that you have received it,** and it will be yours.

Manifestation: the supernatural Gift of Faith is difficult to fully describe; instead, it must be *experienced* to be fully understood. The manifestation of the supernatural Gift of Faith can best be described as the sudden, tangible arrival of a complete calm and quiet assurance which displaces all inner turmoil, doubt, and uncertainty. At such moments, extreme miracles become possible, including the raising of the dead back to life.

In your class instructor Paul's experience, the above scripture (Mark 11:22-24) triggers the release of the Holy Spirit supernatural gift of faith more than any other cause. Here's why: when viewing the dismal outward physical symptoms of a dying terminally ill cancer patient versus this remarkable promise in God's Word, we are presented with a choice: either we can either choose to believe what our physical senses see, hear and smell (example: the awful physical symptoms a dying patient in his/her last days of life), or we can choose to believe God's Word.

Nevertheless, our decision to believe God's Word in and by itself may not be enough to dispel all inner fear and uncertainty with such dismal circumstances in front of us. In such times, by praying in tongues and waiting on the mighty Holy Spirit to move, all at once out the "blue" the supernatural Gift of Faith suddenly arrives and possesses the recipient so completely that all inner uncertainty and fear is instantly replaced by the calm, living, and overpowering assurance of God's absolute power over the natural realm.

This sudden assurance occurs in a muted audio, near-soundless state (a near-trance condition) that is all but impossible to describe. In such moments the most extreme and "impossible" miracles become easy, and unusual manifestations of God's power may sweep an entire audience. This all-but-indescribable state may last on the recipient for several minutes or hours afterwards, or even occasionally for a day or more.

6.4.8 The Gift of Speaking in Tongues

This is the second of three utterance or inspirational gifts:

- 1 Corinthians 12:10 NIV: ...*to another speaking in different kinds of tongues*...

Description: the supernatural Gift of Speaking in Tongues is the ability to speak in one or more languages which the speaker has no natural ability to do on his or her own. These languages may be known as human languages or the unknown languages of angels.

Example:

- Mark 16:17 (Jesus):
  And these signs will accompany those who believe: In my name they will drive out demons; they will speak in new tongues;

- Acts 2:1-4 NIV (example of known languages):

  2 When the day of Pentecost came, they were all together in one place.

  2 Suddenly a sound like the blowing of a violent wind came from heaven and filled the whole house where they were sitting.

  3 They saw what seemed to be tongues of fire that separated and came to rest on each of them.

  4 All of them were filled with the Holy Spirit and **began to speak in other tongues as the Spirit enabled them.**

- 1 Corinthians 14:2-5 NIV (example of unknown languages):

  2 For anyone who speaks in a tongue a does not speak to people but to God. Indeed, **no one understands them; they utter mysteries by the Spirit.**

  3 But the one who prophesies speaks to people for their strengthening, encouraging and comfort.

  4 **Anyone who speaks in a tongue edifies themselves**, but the one who prophesies edifies the church.

  5 I would like every one of you to speak in tongues, but I would rather have you prophesy. The one who prophesies is greater than the one who speaks in tongues, **unless someone interprets**, so that the church may be edified.

Manifestation: The Gift of Speaking in Tongues requires two separate parties to work together, namely the Holy Spirit and us. If we will not open our mouths to give the utterance, then the Holy Spirit cannot speak known or unknown languages through us.

Yet on the one hand, if we speak without the supernatural utterance of the Holy Spirit through our lips, then all we are speaking is our own made-up gibberish. What a beautiful miraculous quandary!

Caution: when we speak tongues by the power of the Holy Spirit, you will not know what you are speaking until you hear it coming out of your mouth. So if you know what you are about to speak before you say it, then this means *you* are the one doing the speaking – if so, do not fret – commit to starting over with Lesson 1 in this book seeking the fullness of the indwelling of the Holy Spirit as evidenced in the speaking of tongues.

_____

_____

_____

6.4.9 The Gift of Interpretation of Tongues

This is the third of three utterance or inspirational gifts:

- 1 Corinthians 12:10 NIV: *...and to still another the **interpretation of tongues***

Description: the Gift of Interpretation of Tongues is the supernatural ability to hear someone (or even yourself) speaking in tongues and translate it into understandable human speech.
Example:

- 1 Corinthians 14:5 NIV:
  I would like every one of you to speak in tongues, but I would rather have you prophesy. The one who prophesies is greater than the one who speaks in tongues, **unless someone interprets**, so that the church may be edified.

Manifestation: as heard by someone blessed by the Holy Spirit with the Gift of Interpretation of Tongues, he or she may not always be aware that someone is speaking in tongues, because as perceived by them what they may hear is only God's Words spoken in plain English (or other applicable native language). So, the Gift of Speaking in Tongues and the Gift of Interpretation of Tongues when combined are the same as the simple Gift of Prophecy (covered previously).

_____

_____

_____

_____

6.5 Comparing the Navi vs. Seer Prophetic Giftings

There are two different prophetic anointings that the Holy Spirit gives to the church. The first and most dominant by far is the "**navi**" prophetic gift, and the second is the far less common and often misunderstood "**seer**" prophetic gift.
Explanation: the Hebrew word for prophet (**nāvî**) means *"spokesman, to proclaim, to call, summon,"* while the Hebrew words ra'ah, ro'e, and ḥoze all mean "**seer**" as used in 1 Samuel 9:19, meaning *"to see or perceive secret and hidden things."*

Unfortunately, those who have the navi prophetic gift often misunderstand, doubt, or envy (or all three!) those who have the seer prophetic gift. Meanwhile, those who have the seer prophetic gift often envy or resent (or both!) those who have the navi prophetic gift.

To help close this divide, both sides should remember that the Holy Spirit alone gives different gifts to different ones as He sovereignly so decides:

- 1 Corinthians 12:11 NLT:
  It is the one and only Spirit who distributes all these gifts. **He alone decides which gift each person should have.**

For best effect, <u>both</u> prophetic giftings are needed to optimally serve the needs of church. To help illustrate this, here is a short, simplistic comparison of characteristics of these two quite different prophetic giftings.

- **The Navi prophetic gifting:**
  - ~97% majority dominance among prophetic anointings.
  - -Revelation typically occurs on the spot of its need, or in response to prayer, or by taking a step of faith to begin speaking.
  - Revelation is received most commonly by impressions, thoughts, and/or the voice of the Holy Spirit audible in their spirits or minds.
  - Revelation may also be received through dreams at night or a daytime flash of a visual image, or even a short vision.

- **The Seer prophetic gifting:**
  - ~3% minority occurrence among prophetic anointings.
  - -Revelation typically comes in advance of need, often the night before; rarely occurs on the spot of need or in response to prayer.
  - -Revelation is received most commonly by experiencing (living) the emotions and feelings of others nearby or far away, always in real time.
  - -Revelation is also commonly received by brief visual flashes, vivid dreams at night and startling visions by day; often experience past, present and future events first person on scene, or may even be transported to a distant location through an out-of-body experience. The prophets Samuel and Ezekiel in the Bible were both seers with radical vision – see 1 Samuel 10:1-8; Ezekiel 1:1-25; Ezekiel 2:1-2; 3:14-15; and especially Ezekiel 8:1-4 coupled with Ezekiel 11:24-35).

When believers with the navi and seer prophetic giftings decide to work together instead of pulling apart or ignoring each other, the strengths of both mesh together work for the substantial heightened benefit for the church.

For example, in a single hour in a church prayer booth those with the navi prophetic gifting may prophesy to dozens of the needy on the spot. Meanwhile, although their seer prophetic companions may only prophesy to a single person during that time span, it can be a life-changing event for the recipient due to the startling depth and meticulous details that are typically produced from the seer gifting.

By the two prophetic streams working together in harmony, the body of Christ can experience the fullness of prophetic revelation as designed by the Holy Spirit.

_____

_____

_____

_____

6.6 Prophetic Giftings vs. Prophets

What is the difference between someone with a prophetic gifting and someone who is a prophet?

First of all, the Apostle Paul gave us a clue into the answer:

- 1 Corinthians 14:1 NIV:
  Follow the way of love and eagerly desire gifts of the Spirit, especially prophecy.

While every believer can learn to hear the voice of God and in time the majority if not all can prophesy, most of us would agree that this does not make every such believer a prophet.

However, some of God' servants walk in a prophetic anointing that is so consistent, accurate, and effective that one or more of Jesus' churches have chosen to recognize that person with the descriptive label of *prophetic* (only as a description; this should never be a title!).

_____

_____

_____

_____

6.7 Do not Worship Gifts, Worship Jesus

The Holy Spirit does give us as individual members of Jesus' church various combinations of spiritual gifts as He (the Holy Spirit) so decides. We then must identify, treasure, use, and grow these gifts, as stated here:

- 1 Corinthians 12:11 NIV:
  All these are the work of one and the same Spirit, **and He distributes them to each one, just as He determines.**

- 1 Timothy 4:14 NIV:
  Do not neglect your gift, which was given you through prophecy when the body of elders laid their hands on you.

However, while these two facts are true, it is also equally true that our focus must remain on Jesus, not on our individual gifts.

For the full video recorded testimony, see page 5.

Illustrative Testimony:
Author's experience of what happened when he attempted to consciously use his Holy Spirit given gift of healing.

_____

_____

_____

_____

6.8 Spooky Coincidences vs. Waiting on the Holy Spirit

Omen - an event regarded as a portent of good or evil; of prophetic significance: "the raven seemed a bird of evil omen" -Oxford dictionary.

If we believers use omens ("spooky coincidences") to guide our lives, sadly there is little separating us from those who practice demonic fortune-telling.

The Word of God has this directive (multiple translations):

- Leviticus 19:26b NIV: Do not practice divination or seek omens.

- Leviticus 19:26b AMP: You shall not... practice divination [using omens or witchcraft] or soothsaying.

- Leviticus 19:26b GW: ...Never cast evil spells, and never consult fortunetellers.

- Leviticus 19:26b NLT: ... Do not practice fortune-telling or witchcraft.

Nevertheless, some Christians nevertheless allow their lives to be guided by coincidences and numerology rather than by God's Word and the prophetic direct guidance of the Holy Spirit alone.

Oddly, even some Spirit-filled believers who faithfully read their Bibles, speak in tongues, and hear from the Holy Spirit nevertheless still allow themselves to be led in every direction by numerology and coincidences.

As an example, if such believers see a red camera in a dream, upon awakening they may become excited when they see a red Camaro to the point they may even attempt to track it down or follow it. Days, weeks, or months later they may still be excitedly talking about their various chance coincidences with red Camaros and their owners.

These believers likewise treat numbers and the analysis of same with the same high enthusiasm – even though neither can be seen in the Bible even once as sources of guidance for Jesus or His apostles. Even worse, many of these believers spend much more of their time excitedly talking about the many coincidences they continually notice than they ever do about Jesus or sound Bible teaching.

Sadly, it can be an exceedingly difficult habit for these believers to break their fascination with numerology and coincidences. A major reason why seems to be because little or no waiting on the Holy Spirit is needed to find what these deceived people believe is "guidance" from God. Another reason often seems to be their self-gratification over the attention and mental effort that is needed to successfully track, analyze, decipher, and "connect" such coincidences.

Waiting on the Holy Spirit to reveal His Will when needed is thrown aside in a favor of an excited rush to try to figure out well in advance what God is going to do and where, why, how and with whom – a set of revelations that we very rarely see in the Bible.

_____

_____

_____

_____

Additional Class Notes (Lesson Six)

Your Personal Notes, Observations, and Class Activities

_____

_____

_____

_____

_____

_____

_____

_____

_____

_____

_____

_____

_____

_____

_____

_____

_____

_____

_____

_____

_____

Questions for the Instructors or the class:

1. _____

_____

_____

_____

_____

_____

2. _____

_____

_____

_____

_____

3. _____

_____

_____

_____

_____

_____

6.9 Walking It Out–Class Assignment (LESSON SIX)

WALKING IT OUT-- Class Assignment (LESSON SIX)

<u>OUR ACTION PLAN</u>

<u>*Seek* **JESUS** at a *level and depth that you may not have previously* to continually further develop and deepen your intimate, personal relationship with Jesus.</u>

Continued Class Action Assignments

Read Daily: "Expect to Believe: 90 Bible Devotionals to Increase Your Faith for the Impossible" by Paul Williams (expect a close encounter with the Holy Spirit to happen while reading these devotionals daily).

Watch / Listen to the Class Lesson Videos; pause when needed to read-pray scriptures, work Action Plan steps, work Homework Challenges and Go Deeper **as** you go through your class notes AGAIN. (*Journaling revelations Holy Spirit has shown you*)

Review Weekly: Key Learning Objectives (*check off each one as you achieve the objectives of this week's lesson (see this chapter's Introduction). Ask the Holy Spirit to plant these objectives deep in your heart and mind and help put them into practice in your daily life.*

Suggested Action: fast, creating an intimate relationship with God: (*per section 1.2 apply the three key takeaways that the author learned*). God responds to fasting and prayer. <u>**Adding a Biblically based food-fast is even better and can aid in combination with God's Word and prayer to a significant breakthrough**</u> (*see section 1.12*) <u>**Speak aloud** the action items in the seven steps taken from James 4:7-10</u> (*especially steps 5& 6 (see section 1.12*)).

Daily abide in the overflow of the anointing of Holy Spirit (*as described in sections 1.5 and 1.6*). Ask the Holy Spirit **every day** to **soften your heart and fill you with God's amazing love** for Your fellow created human beings. Re-commit to earnestly seeking the Holy Ghost in His fullness in your life.

Daily read and apply the books of <u>John, Acts, and Ephesians</u>[19] *(see section 1.12)* using the "read-pray the Word approach and the seven steps to "Intimate Relationship with God"

Always follow the lead of the Holy Spirit! His directions must always immediately displace every plan and course of action of our own. Speak only what the Holy Spirit tells you to.

For a **primer** about **the Holy Spirit**, read-pray the scripture-packed overview of **Appendix A**, "Introduction to the Holy Spirit." *(Journal what is being revealed by the Holy Spirit)*

Re-Read Study and Pray *chapters 6 and 7* "**Gifts of the Holy Spirit**," Parts 1 and 2.

Learn and commit to memory the practical limits of our authority in Christ to cast out demons and to heal the sick and injured. *(see section 5.5)*

Action Assignments for Lesson Six →

Miracle working factors to contemplate again: *"When we believers speak God's Word boldly with our lips in the name of Jesus through the Holy Spirit's power indwelling within us, the result is signs, wonders, and miracles for the glory of God."*

Faith versus Bravado: Speaking *forcefully* or *loudly* is neither important nor helpful in working a miracle, however, speaking *boldly* <u>always</u> is *(whether in a loud or quiet voice)*. This is because speaking *forcefully* typically is a manifestation of our *emotions*, whereas speaking with *boldness* is a manifestation our *faith*.

Eagerly desire the greater **gifts of the Holy Spirit** *(Commit to treasuring, using, and growing these gifts)*

Do not guide your life by personal prophecies. *The Word and the Spirit always agree:* never accept a personal prophecy from anyone without first confirming it directly with the Word of God <u>and</u> the Holy Spirit, in that order *(see section 6.4.1)*.

As followers of Jesus, we all must make sure that our attention is not excessively focused on the flashy nine (9) Gifts of the Holy Spirit in 1 Corinthians while

---

[19] In our observation, no other combination of three books in the Bible gives as much spiritual return for the time expended. These three books serve as an effective jumping point to read-pray the remainder of the entire Bible.

overlooking of the all-important, foundational nine (9) Fruits of the Holy Spirit in Galatians chapter 5:22-23.

Honestly ask yourself if each of these fruits are displayed in your life in <u>ever-increasing measure</u>… and if not, prayerfully ask the Holy Spirit as to why not and what is the appropriate corrective remedy.

Carefully study Galatians 5:22-23 and prayerfully meditate on each fruit, one-by-one.

HOMEWORK CHALLENGE

1. What two things are we to guide our lives by?

_____

_____

_____

2. Why is it important to have clear knowledge of the fruit and gifts of the Holy Spirit? Why should we yearn to possess or be filled with the fruits and the gifts of the Holy Spirit?

_____

_____

_____

_____

3. When does the first characteristics of God start to show in our character? How does this come about?

_____

_____

_____

_____

4. What are revelation gifts? What are the similarities and differences between them? What makes each one unique?

_____

_____

_____

_____

_____

_____

5. Name three spiritual gifts that require action performed on our part. Describe the action required of us for each gift.

_____

_____

_____

_____

_____

What are the similarities and differences between each spiritual gift's manifestation?

_____

_____

_____

_____

_____

6. When our natural gift of faith runs short of performing a miracle, what four areas may require a **supernatural gift of faith**? What two actions should we take when faced with dismal circumstances that require a supernatural gift of faith?

_____

_____

_____

_____

_____

7. What are the three utterance or inspirational gifts? What are the similarities and differences between them? What makes each one unique?

_____

_____

_____

_____

_____

_____

8. Expound on the comparison of the Navi and Seer prophetic giftings. Give a description of why those with these different prophetic gifts are tempted with division?

_____

_____

_____

_____

_____

9. How do you personally feel about Christians who use the prophetic for themselves?

_____

_____

_____

_____

_____

10. What does the Word of God say about omens?

_____

_____

_____

GOING DEEPER (Journal Time)

1. What do you need to do to increase the measure of the Holy Spirit fruit in your life to be effective and productive in your knowledge of Christ? What fruit do you need to improve? Prayerfully ask the Holy Spirit why and what is the appropriate corrective remedy.

_____

_____

_____

2. Why did prophecy change between the old and new testaments?

_____

_____

_____

3. What are the seven ways the Word of Knowledge and the Word of Wisdom manifest? What are the differences between the two? Why is this important?

_____

_____

_____

4. What gifts of the Holy Spirit are operating in your life? Which gift (s) do you operate in more than others? (The gift of discernment, prophecy, interpretation of tongues, etc.) Based on what observations and the Word from God?

_____

_____

_____

7

Gifts of the Holy Spirit, Part 2 of 2

TODAY'S LESSON 7 IS THE highlight event of our 10-week long Bible class series. This evening, we will continue last week's introductory "Gifts of the Holy Spirit, Part 1 of 2" lesson with Part 2. This evening we will conduct a careful case history dissection of some of the most intense and astonishing on-the-spot signs, wonders, and miracles that your class instructors personally have ever been a part of.

We will do this for four reasons:

1) We will review each of the 9 Gifts of the Holy Spirit individually one-by-one to learn many behind-the-scenes important lessons from both the successes and failures of your class instructors.

2) Examine the 9 Gifts from a Biblical perspective to learn how Holy-Spirit-filled believers can attain and maintain the level of faith in God and His Word that is needed to consistently do such miracles, as Jesus said we would (see John 14:12, 13).

3) Learn additional ways of dealing with difficult healing scenarios as important follow up to our prior lesson on this subject in Lesson 5 in this book entitled, *"Handling Problematic Situations.*

4) Stir you to "Godly jealousy" (*"if fasting and prayer worked for them, well then Lord I'll pursue that gift the same way!"*).

7.1 Signs, Wonders, & Miracles of the Holy Spirit

First, for our convenient reference purposes here is the Bible's list of the 9 Gifts of the Holy Spirit again:

- 1 Corinthians 12:7-11 NIV: (reference scripture)

  7 Now to each one the manifestation of the Spirit is given for the common good.

  8 To one there is given through the Spirit **a message of wisdom**, to another a **message of knowledge** by means of the same Spirit,

  9 to another **faith** by the same Spirit, to another **gifts of healing** by that one Spirit,

  10 to another **miraculous powers**, to another **prophecy**, to another **distinguishing between spirits**, to another **speaking in different kinds of tongues**, and to still another the **interpretation of tongues**.

  11 All these are the work of one and the same Spirit, and He distributes them to each one, just as He determines.

7.1.1 "Extreme" Personal Testimonies

Illustrative Testimonies: Sit back and enjoy a joint presentation by your class instructors. We will review each of the 9 Gifts of the Holy Spirit one-by-one in the same order these gifts were initially examined in last week's class. Each gift of the Holy Spirit will be illustrated with first person testimonies of signs, wonders, and miracles… and including our pitfalls, doubts, and errors, too.

 Our goal through this is for you to understand how each of these gifts work and how we can utilize them most effectively in our individual ministries and daily lives. We will also learn better how to deal with the inner uncertainties, doubts, unexpected outcomes, regrets, missed opportunities, tests, attacks, and failures that we all experience at some point or another.

7.1.2 Testimonies: Prophecy

Recap from the prior chapter: the "simple gift of prophecy" may be thought of as God's heart for us, rather than specific revelation about past, current or future events. The gift of prophecy is often life transformative and means much more for far longer than does the flashier revelation gifts of the Word of Knowledge and Word of Wisdom, which are revelation about specific past, current or future events or situations.

- 1 Corinthians 14:1, 3 NIV: (reference scripture)

  1 Desire earnestly spiritual gifts, **but especially that you may prophesy**

  […]

  3 But the one who prophesies speaks to people for their **strengthening, encouraging** and **comfort**.

- Jeremiah 23:29 NIV:

  "Is not **my word like fire**," declares the Lord, "and like a **hammer** that breaks a rock in pieces?

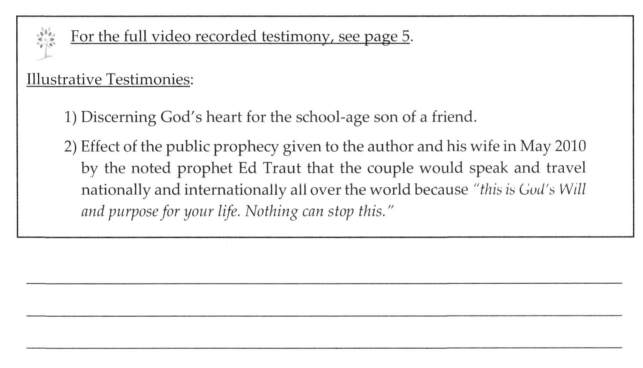

For the full video recorded testimony, see page 5.

Illustrative Testimonies:

1) Discerning God's heart for the school-age son of a friend.

2) Effect of the public prophecy given to the author and his wife in May 2010 by the noted prophet Ed Traut that the couple would speak and travel nationally and internationally all over the world because *"this is God's Will and purpose for your life. Nothing can stop this."*

7.1.3 Testimonies: The Word of Knowledge

Recap from last week: the Word of Knowledge is divine revelation about past or in-progress events.

- 1 Corinthians 12:8 NIV: (reference scripture)

  …to another a **message of knowledge** by means of the same Spirit

For the full video recorded testimony, see page 5.

Illustrative Testimonies:

1) Physical healing of an agnostic student in our secular monthly business class.
2) Story of an accountability partner reaching for a 6-pack of beer.
3) The "Miracle of 3:12 AM."

_____

_____

_____

_____

7.1.4 Testimonies: The Word of Wisdom

Recap from last week: the Word of Wisdom is divine revelation about future events.

- 1 Corinthians 12:8 NIV: (reference scripture)
  To one there is given through the Spirit **a message of wisdom**…

 For the full video recorded testimony, see page 5.

Illustrative Testimonies:

1) "Take the job" testimony.
2) Future events appearing as small running video windows stretching off into the distance (see Amos chapter 7 where God visually previews three different versions of the future!).
3) God promised to fix the author's fear of man "once and for all," followed by stepping through a wall four days into the future.

_____

_____

_____

_____

7.1.5 Testimonies: Discerning of Spirits

Recap from last week: the gift of the Discernment of spirits is supernatural insight through our five physical human senses and/or our human emotions (feelings) into the realm of spirits – specifically, spirits of all three types: angelic spirits, demonic spirits, and human spirits.

- 1 Corinthians 12:10 NIV: (reference scripture)
  …to another distinguishing between spirits…

For the full video recorded testimony, see page 5.

Illustrative Testimonies:

1) Feeling the Presence of the Holy Spirit moving on physical skin.

2) Hearing conversations with physical ears from 200 miles away.

3) Seeing angels and demons with physical eyes.

_____

_____

_____

_____

7.1.6 Testimonies: Gifts of Healing

Recap from last week: the Gifts of Healing is the Holy Spirit-given ability to heal physical disease and ailments.

- 1 Corinthians 12:7-11 NIV: (reference scripture)
to another faith by the same Spirit, to another gifts of healing by that one Spirit,

 <u>For the full video recorded testimony, see page 6.</u>

<u>Illustrative Testimonies</u>

1) Healings at a LGBTQ+ company.

2) Triple-healing of a former U.S. Special Forces solder… followed the next day by his healing from snake bite.

   o Bonus Video Testimony: *"3-Minute Testimony of Healing & Salvation at a 10-Minute Oil Change Shop"* at: <u>https://youtu.be/Dqxd_RXw6_E</u>.

Observation: we have frequently noticed over the years that God heals most non-believers and new Christians at the very <u>start</u> of our prayer for their healing. Scripture reference:

- Isaiah 65:24 NLT (God):
I will answer them before they even call to me. **While they are still talking** about their needs, I will go ahead and answer their prayers!

_____

_____

_____

_____

7.1.7 Testimonies: Working of Miracles

Recap from last week: the Holy Spirit gift of the Working of Miracles is the supernatural ability to perform actions which violate the natural order of things, including the laws of science and physics.

- 1 Corinthians 12:10 NIV: (reference scripture)
  ...to another miraculous powers...

For the full video recorded testimony, see page 5.

Illustrative Testimonies:

1) Car repair miracle; new car makeover.

2) Riding on an invisible airport shuttle bus[20].

3) $10,000 up-front job payment in cash with no receipt required.

4) Commanding a business vice-president not to speak in two different meetings.

5) Swimming pool miracle while witnessing to an ardent atheist.

7.1.8 Testimonies: Gift of Faith

Recap from last week: the Gift of Faith is supernatural faith from God which arrives to supplement our faith when it fades or runs out.

- 1 Corinthians 12:9 NIV: (reference scripture)
  ...to another faith by the same Spirit...

---

[20] Excerpted from Lesson 24, "God Will Perform Miracles for You If You Will Ask" from the book, "Expect to Believe: 90 Bible Devotionals to Increase Your Faith for the Impossible" by Paul Williams published by High Bridge Books.

For the full video recorded testimony, see page 5.

<u>Illustrative Testimony:</u>

    1) Healing of a terribly mangled U.S. missionary to Morocco.

_____

_____

_____

_____

7.1.9 Testimonies: Speaking in Tongues

Recap from last week: the Gift of Tongues is the supernatural ability to speak in a human language which the speaker has not learned or an "unknown language" that is not understood by human beings (possibly the "language of angels" referenced in 1 Cor. 13:1).

- Romans 8:26-27 NLT: (reference scripture)
  26 And the Holy Spirit helps us in our weakness. **For example, we don't know what God wants us to pray for.** But the Holy Spirit prays for us with groanings that cannot be expressed in words.
  27 And the Father who knows all hearts knows what the Spirit is saying, **for the Spirit pleads for us believers in harmony with God's own will.**

 For the full video recorded testimony, see page 5.

<u>Illustrative Testimony:</u>

    1) Big trouble at a consulting job for a large customer.

    2) Extreme healing of a business CEO five states away.

    3) Reminder from the *Story of Zambia* in Lesson 3.

_____

_____

_____

_____

7.1.10 Testimonies: Interpretation of Tongues

Recap from last week: the Holy Spirit Gift of the Interpretation of Tongues is the ability to translate (interpret) the utterance of someone speaking in tongues into understandable speech (i.e., "English" or "Spanish" here in the USA, etc.).

- 1 Corinthians 14:4-5 NIV: (reference scripture)
  4 Anyone who speaks in a tongue edifies themselves, but the one who prophesies edifies the church.
  5 I would like every one of you to speak in tongues, but I would rather have you prophesy. The one who prophesies is greater than the one who speaks in tongues, **unless someone interprets**, so that the church may be edified.

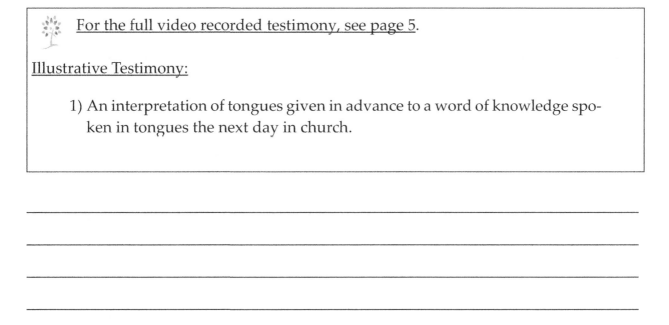

For the full video recorded testimony, see page 5.

Illustrative Testimony:

1) An interpretation of tongues given in advance to a word of knowledge spoken in tongues the next day in church.

_____

_____

_____

_____

Additional Class Notes (Lesson Seven)

Your Personal Notes, Observations, and Class Activities

Questions for the Instructors or the class:

1. _____

_____

_____

_____

_____

2. _____

_____

_____

_____

3. _____

_____

_____

_____

_____

_____

7.2 Walking It Out—Class Assignment (LESSON SEVEN)

WALKING IT OUT -- Class Assignment (LESSON SEVEN)

OUR ACTION PLAN

Seek **JESUS** *at a level and depth that you may not have previously* to continually further develop and deepen your intimate, personal relationship with Jesus.

Continued Class Action Assignments

Read Daily: "Expect to Believe: 90 Bible Devotionals to Increase Your Faith for the Impossible" by Paul Williams (expect a close encounter with the Holy Spirit to happen while reading these devotionals daily).

Watch / Listen to the Class Lesson Videos; pause when needed to read-pray scriptures, work Action Plan steps, work Homework Challenges and Go Deeper **as** you go through your class notes AGAIN. (*Journaling revelations Holy Spirit has shown you*)

Review Weekly: Key Learning Objectives (*check off each one as you achieve the objectives of this week's lesson (see this chapter's Introduction). Ask the Holy Spirit to plant these objectives deep in your heart and mind and help put them into practice in your daily life.*

Suggested Action: fast, creating an intimate relationship with God: (*per section 1.2 apply the three key takeaways that Paul learned*) God responds to fasting and prayer. *Adding a Biblically based food-fast is even better and can aid in combination with God's Word and prayer to a significant breakthrough* (see section 1.12) **Speak aloud the action items in the seven steps taken from James 4:7-10** (*especially steps 5& 6 (see section 1.12)*)

Daily abide in the overflow of the anointing of Holy Spirit (*as described in sections 1.5 and 1.6*). Ask the Holy Spirit **every day** to **soften your heart and fill you with God's amazing love** for Your fellow created human beings. Re-commit to earnestly seeking the Holy Ghost in His fullness in your life.

Daily read and apply the books of _John, Acts, and Ephesians_[21] *(see section 1.12)* using the "read-pray the Word approach" and the "Seven Steps to Intimate Relationship with God."

Always follow the lead of the Holy Spirit! His directions should always displace every plan and course of action of our own.

For a **primer or refresher** about **the Holy Spirit**, read-pray the scripture-packed overview of **Appendix A**, "Introduction to the Holy Spirit." *(Journal what is revealed by the Holy Spirit)*

Re-Read Study and Pray *chapters 6 and 7 "Gifts of the Holy Spirit,"* Parts 1 and 2.

Learn and commit to memory the practical limits of our authority in Christ to cast out demons and to heal the sick and injured. *(see section 5.5).*

Miracle working factors: *"When we believers speak God's Word boldly with our lips in the name of Jesus through the Holy Spirit's power indwelling within us, the result is signs, wonders, and miracles for the glory of God."*

Important: Speaking *forcefully* and/or *loudly* is neither important nor helpful in working a miracle, however, **speaking *boldly* <u>always</u> is (***whether in a loud or quiet voice***). This is because speaking *forcefully* typically is a manifestation of our *emotions*, whereas speaking with *boldness* is a manifestation our *faith*.**

Eagerly desire the greater **gifts of the Holy Spirit** *(We must treasure, use, and grow these gifts).*

Do not guide your life by personal prophecies. *The Word and the Spirit always agree:* never accept a personal prophecy from anyone without first confirming it directly yourself with the Word of God and the Holy Spirit, in that order *(see section 6.4.1).*

As followers of Jesus, we all must make sure that our attention is not excessively focused on the flashy nine (9) Gifts of the Holy Spirit in 1 Corinthians 12:7-11 to the overlooking of the all-important, foundational nine (9) Fruits of the Holy Spirit in Galatians 5:22-23.

---

[21] In our observation, no other combination of three books in the Bible gives as much spiritual return for the time expended. These three books serve as an effective jumping point to real-pray the remainder of the entire Bible.

Honestly ask yourself if each of the Fruits of the Holy Spirit are displayed in your life in ever-increasing measure… and if not, prayerfully ask the Holy Spirit as to why not and what is the appropriate corrective remedy.

Action Assignments for Lesson Seven →

See the actions listed above regarding *the Fruits and the Gifts of the Holy Spirit*

Rewatch and Review lesson seven testimony recordings.

HOMEWORK CHALLENGE

1. While actively listening to each testimony what spiritual insight/ information /or conclusion did you attain from the instructor (s) that helped you to better understand learn how to deal with the inner uncertainties, doubts, unexpected outcomes, regrets, missed opportunities, tests, attacks, and failures?

a. Prophecy?

_____

_____

_____

_____

_____

b. The Word of Knowledge?

_____

_____

_____

_____

c. The Word of Wisdom?

_____

_____

_____

_____

_____

d. Discerning of Spirits?

_____

_____

_____

_____

_____

e. Gifts of Healing?

_____

_____

_____

_____

_____

f. Working of Miracles?

_____

_____

_____

_____

_____

g. Gift of Faith?

_____

_____

_____

_____

_____

h. Speaking in Tongues?

_____

_____

_____

_____

_____

i. Interpretation of Tongues?

_____

_____

_____

_____

_____

GOING DEEPER (Journal Time)

1. After rewatching, reviewing and reflecting on the class instructor testimonies, were you stirred to Godly jealousy? If so, seek the Holy Spirit on how to attain and maintain the level of faith in God and His Word to consistently do such miracles. Be sure to journal your journey!

_____

_____

_____

2. Review and meditate over the meaning of each Gift of the Holy Spirit.

8

Prophetic Accuracy + Gift of "The Knowing"

OUR LEARNING OBJECTIVES for Lesson 8 are:

- Understanding the reasons for prophetic inaccuracy.

- Removing blocks to consistent, accurate prophetic revelation.

- Understanding and utilizing "The Knowing," God's special gift of swift decision-making wisdom for **all** His children.

As usual, we will give testimonies illustrating all lesson objectives over the course of this evening.

8.1 Prophesying with Accuracy

How exactly do errors, omissions, and even major errors creep into prophetic revelation? What are the root causes? And what can each of us do to prevent such errors from occurring in the first place, and detect and fix them if they do occur?

In response, there are three major root cause problems which can interfere with or corrupt our ability to hear accurately from God. Worst yet, they also can result in us hearing lies and delusions of demons instead of God's voice.

What are these three major root cause reasons? They are:

1) Hearing from evil spirits who gain access through unrepented sin to masquerade as God's voice.
2) Hearing from our own error-prone, biased human minds.
3) Distortion caused by serious doctrinal or foundational error.

We will study each of these traps in detail one at a time next.

8.1.1 Barrier 1: Hearing from Evil Spirits

This may come as a shock to you (it should!), but it can be remarkably easy for even deeply experienced Holy Spirit-filled warriors to inadvertently hear the voice of our enemy and yet sincerely but mistakenly believe that the Holy Spirit is the source. In fact, at some point or the other, it is likely that *every* Christian believer will make this mistake at least once.

To understand why, we first need to better understand the inherent nature of our ability to hear from God in the first place. On this subject the Bible is clear that the Gifts of the Holy Spirit --once given-- are never withdrawn from their recipients:

- Romans 11:29 NIV: "for God's gifts and his call are **irrevocable**."

A good example of this in the Bible is the story of misguided prophet Balaam[22]:

- Numbers chapters 22 – 24:
  (Background: an evil Moabite King named Balak attempts to pay a prophet named Balaam to curse God's people Israel – read the full story on your own time in your Bible.)

---

[22] Another disturbing incident in the Bible of a prophet who was hearing from both God and Satan can be found in 1 Kings 13:11-32.

- Numbers 22:5-7 NIV:

  5 (Balak) sent messengers to summon Balaam son of Beor, who was at Pethor, near the Euphrates River, in his native land. Balak said: 'A people has come out of Egypt; they cover the face of the land and have settled next to me.

  6 Now come and put a curse on these people, because they are too powerful for me. Perhaps then I will be able to defeat them and drive them out of the land. **For I know that whoever you bless is blessed, and whoever you curse is cursed.'**

  7 The elders of Moab and Midian left, **taking with them the fee for divination**. When they came to Balaam, they told him what Balak had said.

But although Balaam clearly was willing to accept money to try to put a Satanic curse on God's people Israel, nevertheless God still prophesied anyway through Balaam about the distant future arrival of Jesus, His Son:

- Numbers 24:1-2, 15-17 NIV:

  1 Now when Balaam saw that it pleased the Lord to bless Israel, he did not resort **to divination as at other times** but turned his face toward the wilderness.

  2 When Balaam looked out and saw Israel encamped tribe by tribe, **the Spirit of God came on him**

    […]

  15 Then (Balaam) spoke his message:

  'The prophecy of Balaam son of Beor,

    the prophecy of one whose eye sees clearly,

  16 the prophecy of one **who hears the words of God**,

    who has **knowledge from the Most High**,

  who sees a **vision from the Almighty**,

    who falls prostrate, and whose eyes are opened:

  17 I see him, but not now;

    I behold him, but not near.

  A star will come out of Jacob;

    a scepter will rise out of Israel.

  He will crush the foreheads of Moab,

    the skulls of all the people of Sheth.'

———————————————————————————————

———————————————————————————————

———————————————————————————————

———————————————————————————————

To leave no doubt of how evil Balaam had become, here are more scriptures passages detailing Balaam's greed for money while showing he was clearly speaking for Satan.

- Joshua 13:22 NIV: "In addition to those slain in battle, the Israelites had put to the sword **Balaam** son of Beor, who practiced divination" (<< NLT translation: "**magic**").

- 2 Peter 2:15 NIV:
  They have left the straight way and wandered off to follow the way of Balaam son of Bezer, **who loved the wages of wickedness.**

- Nehemiah 13:2 NIV:
  For (the Ammonites) had not provided the Israelites with food and water in the wilderness. **Instead, they hired Balaam to curse them, though our God turned the curse into a blessing.**

- Numbers 31:16 NIV (Moses):
  "They were the ones (the Midianite women) **who followed Balaam's advice and enticed the Israelites to be unfaithful to the Lord** in the Peor incident, so that a plague struck the Lord's people."

- Revelation 2:14 NIV (Jesus): "Nevertheless, I have a few things against you: There are some among you who hold to the teaching of Balaam, **who taught Balak to entice the Israelites to sin** so that they ate food sacrificed to idols and committed sexual immorality."

So how can this be? How could Balaam speak the words of both God and Satan at the same time?

———————————————————————————————

———————————————————————————————

———————————————————————————————

———————————————————————————————

The most likely explanation is that in the beginning Balaam indeed *was* a true prophet of the Most High God at that time. However, because of an inner love of money (financial greed) which Balaam never overcame (after all, *"money is a root of all kinds of evil"* - 1 Timothy 6:10 NIV), Balaam opened a door for Satan to begin to use as he pleased.

Then after Satan began using Balaam as his sorcery medium, God also continued speaking to Balaam, since God's gifts are never withdrawn once given (see again Romans 11:29 above).

In the end, Balaam was killed for his role in seducing Israel into sexual immorality.

_____

_____

_____

_____

CAUTION: Frankly, Balaam's case should be a stark warning to all of us that just because we hear from God does <u>not</u> mean that we are not also possibly hearing from Satan as well. If we have ongoing sin in our lives of any type that we continue to delay repenting of and overcoming, we can be sure that our adversary the devil *will* notice and *will* attempt to exploit against that individual and God's church through him or her.

 For the full video recorded testimony, see page 5.

Illustrative Testimony: young man hearing from both God and Satan at the same time.

Key takeaway lesson 1: **always** compare **all** <u>parts</u> of **everything** we hear to the scriptures. <u>Never</u> skip this step!

Key takeaway lesson 2: the faster we attain a comprehensive and accurate deep understanding of the entire Word of God for ourselves, the better!

Finally, as a general but reliable guide to help us begin the process determining which voice is which, the nature of our loving Father God can be summarized by these characteristics. God asks us to:

- *Wait* on Him to act.
- Have faith that He hears us and will respond.
- Trust in Him and His Word the Bible with our words and actions.

The nature of our enemy can also be characterized. Satan inspires:

- Hasty decisions (*"you'll never this opportunity again. Don't wait, do it now!"*).

- Searching for secret or exclusive knowledge that few others have.

- Superior, prideful, or individualistic thinking (*"Finally! I get do it my way!"*).

_____

_____

_____

_____

8.1.2 Barrier 2: Hearing from Our Own Biased Minds

The second major reason for prophetic error is our own misguided thinking, biases, misbeliefs, and eccentric whims in our mentality, thinking and conduct toward others.

The erroneous impact that our own evil human natures can have on prophecy is explained well by this scripture passage:

- Titus 1:15 NIV:
  To the pure, all things are pure, but to those who are corrupted and do not believe, nothing is pure. In fact, both their minds and consciences are corrupted.

This scripture indicates two things relative to prophetic accuracy, namely:

- **Jesus prophesied perfectly accurately every single time:** because Jesus never sinned (Hebrews 4:15). Because His mind was perfectly pure, He was able to hear from our Father God perfectly without distortion or error.

- **We believers prophesy inaccurately at least a portion of the time:** because we "all have sinned and come short of the glory of God" (Romans 3:23), our minds are not perfectly pure, which can result in us not hearing from our Father perfectly.

The more impure and separated from the Word of God are minds are, the more our prophetic accuracy decreases in both substance and frequency.

Here are several examples of how our mental errors and biases directly affect how we hear from God:

- If we are **judgmental**, then what we hear from God will be skewed toward their need for repentance and thoughts of their judgement if they do not.

- If we are **tolerant** toward the sins of others, then what we hear from God will be skewed toward "tolerance" and "love."

- It we are **impatient**, then what we hear from God will be skewed toward pressure and haste (*"time's up, get this done now!"*).

- If we are struggling with **unbelief** ((believing all of God's promises is diffi cult for us), then we will speak the promises of God we hear for others with hesitancy or even not at all.

- If we are secretly treasuring **known sin** in our hearts, then we will minimize or fail to speak to others what we hear from God about these same sins.

Bottomline: the fewer and smaller our internal biases, unbelief, grudges, hang-ups, eccentric thinking, and complaints we have in life (translation: the more like Jesus we grow to become), the more accurately we will hear from God and speak to others.

Our potential for prophetic error is one of the reasons why we should accept -in fact, *solicit*--- the input and oversight of other believers who have a confirmed gift of accurate prophecy:

- 1 Corinthians 14:32 NIV:
The spirits of prophets are subject to the control of prophets.

So how can we become like Jesus? By the constant washing of our minds through our daily prayerful contemplative emersion in God's Word:

- Ephesians 5:25, 26 NIV:
  25 Husbands, love your wives, just as Christ loved the church and gave himself up for her
  26 to make her holy, **cleansing her by the washing with water through the word,**

- Hebrews 4:12 NLT:
  For the word of God is alive and powerful. It is sharper than the sharpest two-edged sword, cutting between soul and spirit, between joint and marrow. **It exposes our innermost thoughts and desires.**

- 2 Timothy 3:16-17 NLT:
  16 All Scripture is inspired by God and is **useful to teach us what is true and to make us realize what is wrong** in our lives. It **corrects us** when we are wrong and **teaches us** to do what is right.
  17 God uses it to **prepare and equip his peo**ple to do every good work.

Here is a helpful short self-examination questionnaire[23] which we should all ask ourselves at regular monthly or better intervals:

1) Am I daily studying the Scriptures to hear from God for myself?

2) Am I maintaining a life of prayer?

3) Am I seeking purity, cleansing, and holiness in my life?

4) Am I a worshipful member of a local Christian congregation which believes, regularly practices, and <u>teaches</u> the full doctrines of God's Word, including the Holy Spirit and His Gifts expressed in speaking in tongues, prophecy, physical healing, and the casting out of demons today… not just long ago in the book of Acts in the Bible?

5) Am I committed to seeking and actively maintaining several peer relationships who can and will boldly speak into my life as they see necessary (referring to watchful, honest accountability partners who are able and willing to bring up issues they see)?

---

[23] Questionnaire adapted from *The Seer Expanded Edition: The Prophetic Power of Visions, Dreams and Open Heavens*, by James W. Goll.

If your answer to any of these five questions is "No" (or "I'm not sure"), then you and your family are in danger. If so, we recommend that you immediately make any identified deficiencies a matter of fervent prayer and immediate corrective action.

_____

_____

_____

_____

8.1.3 Barrier 3: Distortion by Serious Foundational Error

The third and worst root cause reason behind prophetic inaccuracy is one or more serious doctrinal, foundational, and/or character errors.

Major issues are pride, haughtiness, and unwillingness to listen to correction no matter how carefully it is worded. Others are lack of daily Bible study and prayer, feeling lofty and superior to others, and attention on attaining desired results rather than on intimacy with Jesus and the Holy Spirit.

A simple, single example of how sinful pride can arise follows. The more God uses us, the easier it can be for us to believe that there is something inherently good about us, who we are, what we do, or how we do it which contributes to God wanting our help. WRONG! If God will speak through a dumb donkey (Numbers 22:28, 30) or through stones in a wall (Habakkuk 2:11) or stones in the pavement (Luke 19:40) or through demon-perverted Balaam (Numbers 24:17), then it should be obvious from these examples that God's use of someone (or something) is not an endorsement of their (or its) lifestyle.

As we have already seen from the sad story of Balaam, just because God chooses to prophesy through us does <u>not</u> mean we do not have binding sins and chronic failure area in our lives, which if uncorrected causes prophetic inaccuracy, open rooms for misuse by the enemy, and in time as the sin continues growing to even cause us to lose our salvation.

Carefully consider this striking warning by Jesus:

- Mathew 7:21-23 NIV:
  21 "Not everyone who says to me, 'Lord, Lord,' will enter the kingdom of heaven, but only the one who **does the will** of my Father who is in heaven.

22 Many will say to me on that day, **'Lord, Lord, did we not prophesy in your name** and in your name drive out demons and, in your name, perform many miracles?'

23 Then I will tell them plainly, 'I never knew you. Away from me, **you evil-doers!'**

_____

_____

_____

_____

What we invest in God is what we receive back from Him, as shown in this scripture passage:

- Psalm 18:24-27 NLT:

  24 The Lord rewarded me for doing right. He has seen my innocence.

  25 To the faithful you show yourself faithful; to those with integrity you show integrity.

  26 To the pure you show yourself pure, **but to the crooked you show yourself shrewd.**

  27 You rescue the humble, but you humiliate the proud.

This scripture passage explains why and how God can and will use anyone to accomplish His purposes here on earth, no matter how flawed or fatally flawed... which means once again that we must not consider our prophesy and miracles to be God's stamp of approval of all our beliefs and actions.

_____

_____

_____

_____

 CAUTION: Prophetic revelation --no matter how intense, frequent, and informative it may be at times-- is not a substitute for the daily "hungry" study of God's Word.

The Holy Spirit infrequently corrects us through direct prophetic revelation (gasp!). Why? This is because identifying problems and corrective action is one of the major roles of God's Word the Bible in our daily lives, as stated here:

- 2 Timothy 3:16-17 NLT:
  All **Scripture** is inspired by God and **is useful to teach us what is true and to make us realize what is wrong in our lives.**
  17 **It corrects us** when we are wrong and **teaches us** to do what is right. God uses **it** to prepare and equip his people to do every good work.

_____

_____

_____

_____

Summary: just because we are hearing from God and/or doing signs, wonders and miracles in the name of Jesus does not mean we are exempt from the vital instruction, correction, and exhortation of God's Word. Rather, the opposite is true: *because* we are hearing from God and/or doing signs, wonders, and miracles, we *need* God's corrective Word in our lives more than ever.

Let us all once again re-commit to our daily, meaningful, prayerful, "hungry" study of God's Word the Bible… always first for ourselves, then for others.

_____

_____

_____

_____

8.2 "The Knowing," God's Gift of Wisdom

To properly introduce this important but little understood and seldom recognized --or utilized—gift of "The Knowing" from God, we will begin our study of this important subject in the Old Testament:

- Exodus 28:15, 30 NLT (God to Moses):

  15 Then, with great skill and care, make a chestpiece to be **worn for seeking a decision from God.** Make it to match the ephod, using finely woven linen embroidered with gold and with blue, purple, and scarlet thread.

  [...]

  30 Insert **the Urim and Thummim into the sacred chestpiece** so they will be carried over Aaron's heart when he goes into the Lord's presence. In this way, Aaron will always carry over his heart **the objects used to determine the Lord's will** for his people whenever he goes in before the Lord.

- Leviticus 8:8 NIV:

  (Moses) placed the breastpiece on (Aaron) and put the **Urim and Thummim** in the breastpiece.

- Numbers 27:21 NIV (God to Moses):

  (Joshua) is to stand before Eleazar the priest, **who will obtain decisions for him by inquiring of the Urim before the Lord.** At his command he and the entire community of the Israelites will go out, and at his command they will come in.

- 1 Samuel 28:6 NIV:

  (Saul) inquired of the Lord, but the Lord did not answer him by dreams **or Urim** or prophets.

- 1 Samuel 23:9-13 NLT (how God saved David and his men):

  9 But David learned of Saul's plan and told Abiathar the **priest to bring the ephod and ask the Lord what he should do.**

  10 Then David prayed, 'O Lord, God of Israel, I have heard that Saul is planning to come and destroy Keilah because I am here.

  11 Will the leaders of Keilah betray me to him? And will Saul actually come as I have heard? O Lord, God of Israel, please tell me.'

  And the Lord said, 'He will come.'

  12 Again David asked, 'Will the leaders of Keilah betray me and my men to Saul?'

  And the Lord replied, 'Yes, they will betray you.'

13 So David and his men—about 600 of them now—left Keilah and began roaming the countryside. Word soon reached Saul that David had escaped, so he didn't go to Keilah after all.

- Nehemiah 2:63 NIV (genealogy dispute):
The governor ordered them not to eat any of the most sacred food until there was a priest ministering **with the Urim and Thummim.**

_____

_____

_____

_____

8.2.1 Is "The Knowing" Actually God's Wisdom?

Let us study this scripture passage from Proverbs:

- Proverbs 9:9-10 NIV:
9 Instruct the wise and **they will be wiser still**;
    teach the righteous and **they will add to their learning.**
10 The fear of the Lord **is the beginning of wisdom,**
    and knowledge of the Holy One **is understanding.**

This "knowledge upon knowledge" effect or what might be termed "compounded knowledge" is vividly illustrated here:

- Exodus 31:1-5 NIV:
1 Then the Lord spoke to Moses, saying:
2 'See, **I have called by name Bezalel** the son of Uri, the son of Hur, of the tribe of Judah.
3 **And I have filled him with the Spirit of God, in wisdom, in understanding, in knowledge, and in all manner of workmanship,**
4 to design artistic works, to work in gold, in silver, in bronze,
5 in cutting jewels for setting, in carving wood, and to work in all manner of workmanship.'

Bezalel may not have been aware that the hand of God had been upon his entire life until the day God called him through Moses. No doubt before this point Bezalel, his family, and friends all believed that he was simply really, really, *really* good at his work through his own efforts at learning.

But when God's call came, all at once a thousand unexplained incidents in Bezalel's life all became clear to him: it had been God's hand on him powerfully guiding his life and teaching him the entire time. What a revelation!

_____

_____

_____

_____

8.2.2 The Inward Witness

A close but noticeably slower variant of The Knowing is often called, "The Inward Witness." This is the distinct sensation of experiencing "peace" or "loss of peace" in response to contemplated actions or decisions of virtually all types and kinds.

Here are two scripture passages which describes this best:

- Matthew 10:12-13 NIV (Jesus):
  12 As you enter the home, give **it** your greeting.
  13 If the home is deserving, let **your peace** rest on it; if it is not, let your peace return to you.

- Philippians 4:7 NIV:
  "And the peace of God, which transcends all understanding, will guard your hearts and your minds in Christ Jesus."

_____

_____

_____

_____

8.2.3 Examples of The Knowing in the Bible

- Genesis 22:1-5 NIV:

  1 Some time later God tested Abraham. He said to him, "Abraham!" "Here I am," he replied.

  2 Then God said, "Take your son, your only son, whom you love—Isaac—and go to the region of Moriah. Sacrifice him there as a burnt offering on a mountain I will show you."

  3 Early the next morning Abraham got up and loaded his donkey. He took with him two of his servants and his son Isaac. When he had cut enough wood for the burnt offering, he set out for the place God had told him about.

  4 On the third day Abraham looked up and saw the place in the distance. {Paul: he immediately *realized* this is the place]

  5 He said to his servants, "Stay here with the donkey while I and the boy go over there. We will worship and then we will come back to you."

In New Testament of the Bible, the equivalent of the Old Testament's Urim and Thummim appears to be what is often referred to by those who regularly operate in this gift as "The Knowing" or its closely related but slower variant which some call "The Inward Witness" (covered next).

Jesus appears to have regularly operated in the gift of The Knowing, as illustrated in the following scriptures:

- Mark 2:6-9 NLT:

  6 But some of the teachers of religious law who were sitting there thought to themselves,

  7 'What is he saying? This is blasphemy! Only God can forgive sins!

  8 Jesus **knew immediately** what they were thinking, so he asked them, 'Why do you question this in your hearts? '

- Matthew 8:4 NIV:

  Knowing the (scribes') thoughts, Jesus said, 'Why do you entertain evil thoughts in your hearts?'

- Matthew 12:25 NLT:

  Jesus **knew** (the Pharisees' thoughts) and replied, 'Any kingdom divided by civil war is doomed. A town or family splintered by feuding will fall apart.'

- Luke 9:47 NIV:
  Jesus, **knowing their thoughts**, took a little child and had him stand beside him.

- Mark 13:11 NIV (Jesus):
  Whenever you are arrested and brought to trial, do not worry beforehand about what to say. **Just say whatever is given you at the time**, for it is not you speaking, but the Holy Spirit.

Of course, if Jesus did it, so can we (see Lesson 2).

8.2.4 Who Has the Gift of The Knowing

All Christians --and in fact even many honorable, upright, and considerate non-Christians as well-- have the Godly wisdom gift of The Knowing to various degrees, although typically both are unaware they have this gift from God. Why non-Christians? The following Words of Jesus provide some indication of why:

- Psalms 145:9 NIV:
  The Lord is good to all; he has compassion on all he has made.

- Matthew 5:45 NIV (Jesus):
  He (God) causes His sun to rise on the evil and the good, and sends rain on the righteous and the unrighteous.

8.2.5 "The Knowing" vs. Prophetic Revelation

So we can understand the differences, let us compare the wisdom gift of "The Knowing" to the Holy Ghost's prophetic revelation gift of the Word of Knowledge and also to ordinary human guesswork:

- "The Knowing" is instant, but general and unexplainable. No reason whatsoever can be identified as to why this information is known **concurrent with its need**. In fact, to the recipient, it is exactly as if he/or she had always known this information all along, except they become aware that they did not know this information until it was asked or a situation arose that required it.

- The Holy Ghost revelation gift of the Word of Knowledge is specific, but also generally considerably slower, or at times may not be in operation at all.

Our own human guesswork can be near immediate or may come after a few seconds or longer time of pondering. It can always be traced back (perhaps with some effort and time) to our own logical thought processes or our own memories of prior and likely events or to our own individual preexisting notions and biases.

8.2.6 Stick Close to God and His Word

 CAUTION: Exactly just the same as can happen with the 9 Gifts of the Holy Spirit in 1 Corinthians chapter 12, in a similar way God's gift of "The Knowing" can result from and/or be impacted by:

a) The Holy Spirit;

b) Our own inaccurate, incomplete, biased, or perverse thinking,

c) By our enemy the devil.

Thankfully, the same preventative remedies described earlier in this lesson which enable prophetic accuracy also work equally well to safeguard the value and fidelity of The Knowing.

8.2.7 How to Develop "The Knowing"

First, pray for the Holy Spirit's instruction and guidance in the name of Jesus. Then, operating in faith, test and develop this gift in a shopping mall or large store.

(A class exercise assignment with instructions will now be given by your class instructors – see page 5)

Reminder: we must *act* in faith to develop this gift!

_____

_____

_____

_____

8.2.8 Testimonies About "The Knowing":

For the full video recorded testimony, see page 5.

Testimony 1: Which cab should I take to the airport?

Testimony 2: Looking for someone to pray for in a Kroger store, only to unexpectedly end up being the surprise answer to a miracle request in a nearby Taco Bell.

Testimony 3: Super-speedy answers during a job interview led to the interviewers asking hard questions and then a big problem.

Testimony 4: Personal and business phone calls made at precisely the right moment (a regular witnessing opportunity!).

_____

_____

_____

_____

_____

_____

_____

Additional Class Notes (Lesson Eight)

Your Personal Notes, Observations, and Class Activities

_____

_____

_____

_____

_____

_____

_____

_____

_____

_____

_____

_____

_____

_____

_____

_____

_____

_____

_____

_____

Questions for the Instructors or the class:

1. _____

_____

_____

_____

_____

2. _____

_____

_____

_____

_____

3. _____

_____

_____

_____

_____

_____

8.3 Walking It Out -- Class Assignment (LESSON EIGHT)

WALKING IT OUT   Class Assignment (LESSON EIGHT)

OUR ACTION PLAN

Seek **JESUS** at a *level and depth that you may not have previously* to continually further develop and deepen your intimate, personal relationship with Jesus.

Continued Class Action Assignments

Read Daily: "Expect to Believe: 90 Bible Devotionals to Increase Your Faith for the Impossible" by Paul Williams (expect a close encounter with the Holy Spirit to happen while reading these devotionals daily).

Watch / Listen to the Class Lesson Videos; pause when needed to read-pray scriptures, work Action Plan steps, work Homework Challenges and Go Deeper **as** you go through your class notes AGAIN. (*Journaling revelations Holy Spirit has shown you*)

Review Weekly: Key Learning Objectives (*check off each one as you achieve the objectives of this week's lesson (see this chapter's Introduction). Ask the Holy Spirit to plant these objectives deep in your heart and mind and help put them into practice in your daily life.*

Suggested Action: fast, creating an intimate relationship with God: (*per section 1.2 apply the three key takeaways that the author learned*). God responds to fasting and prayer. *Adding a Biblically based food-fast is even better and can aid in combination with God's Word and prayer to a significant breakthrough* (see section 1.12) *Speak aloud* **the action items in the seven steps taken from James 4:7-10** (*especially steps 5& 6 (see section 1.12)*).

Daily abide in the overflow of the anointing of Holy Spirit (*as described in sections 1.5 and 1.6*). Ask the Holy Spirit **every day** to **soften your heart and fill you with God's amazing love** for Your fellow created human beings. Re-commit to earnestly seeking the Holy Ghost in His fullness in your life.

Daily read and apply the books of _John, Acts, and Ephesians_[24] *(see section 1.12)* using the "read-pray the Word approach and the seven steps to "Intimate Relationship with God"

Always follow the lead of the Holy Spirit! His directions must always immediately displace every plan and course of action of our own. Speak only what the Holy Spirit tells you to.

For a primer or refresher about the Holy Spirit, read-pray the scripture-packed overview in **Appendix A**, "Introduction to the Holy Spirit" *(journal what is revealed by the Holy Spirit).*

Re-Read Study and Pray *chapters 6 and 7 "**Gifts of the Holy Spirit**," Parts 1 and 2.*

Learn and commit to memory the practical limits of our authority in Christ to cast out demons and to heal the sick and injured. *(see section 5.5)*

Miracle working factors: *"When we believers speak God's Word boldly with our lips in the name of Jesus through the Holy Spirit's power indwelling within us, the result is signs, wonders, and miracles for the glory of God."*

Important: Speaking *forcefully* and/or *loudly* is neither important nor helpful in working a miracle, however, **speaking *boldly* <u>always</u> is (***whether in a loud or quiet voice*). **This is because speaking** *forcefully* **typically is a manifestation of our** *emotions*, **whereas speaking with** *boldness* **is a manifestation our** *faith.*

Eagerly desire the greater **gifts of the Holy Spirit** *(You must treasure, use, and grow these gifts)*

Do not guide your life by personal prophecies. *The Word and the Spirit always agree.* Never accept a personal prophecy from anyone without first confirming it directly yourself with the Word of God and the Holy Spirit, in that order. *(see section 6.4.1)*

As followers of Jesus, we all must make sure that our attention is not excessively focused on the flashy nine (9) Gifts of the Holy Spirit in 1 Corinthians 12:7-11 to

---

[24] In our observation, no other combination of three books in the Bible gives as much spiritual return for the time expended. These three books serve as an effective jumping point to read-pray the remainder of the entire Bible.

the overlooking of the all-important, foundational nine (9) Fruits of the Holy Spirit in Galatians 5:22-23

Honestly ask yourself if each of the Fruits of the Holy Spirit are displayed in your life in ever-increasing measure… and if not, prayerfully ask the Holy Spirit as to why not and what is the appropriate corrective remedy.

Action Assignments for Lesson Eight →

Take the self-examination questionnaire *(see section 8.1.2)* and make it a regular part of your lifestyle. *Refer back to it frequently.*

Study and thoroughly understand the differences between prophetic revelation from God, The Knowing, and our own human guesswork *(see sections 8.2.5 and 8.2.6).*

Ask the Holy Spirit for instruction and guidance to develop "The Knowing."

Repeat from an earlier lesson's homework assignment - apply this exhortation again for this coming week:

Ephesians 6:18 NIV:
18 **And pray in the Spirit on all occasions** with all kinds of prayers and requests. With this in mind, be alert and always keep on praying for all the Lord's people.

HOMEWORK CHALLENGE

1. When seeking to verify that what you hear is God's voice, in addition to matching every portion of everything you hear with God's Word, what are the characteristics of the nature of God and what are the characteristic of the nature of the enemy?

_____

_____

_____

_____

_____

2. Has there been a time when you were not sure about the voice you were hearing? Or in the past have you heard from what you sincerely believed at the time was God, but you now are questioning? What would you do differently now?

_____

_____

_____

_____

3. What are the three major causes of prophetic error?

_____

_____

_____

_____

4. What we invest in God is what we receive back from Him, so what are your investments? Expound on this question in your own words *(reference the scriptures in section 8.1.3).*

_____

_____

_____

_____

5. In your words and understanding of the Gift of the Knowing *(the inward witness)*, expound on why Christians as well as some non-Christians can operate in this gift. Now after studying and reflecting on the reference scriptures, explain a time when God allowed you to use the Knowing gift. If this applies, at that time did you become aware you were using the gift of the Knowing?

_____

_____

_____

_____

_____

GOING DEEPER (Journal Time)

1. The more impure and separated from the Word of God our minds are, the more our prophetic accuracy decreases in both scriptural substance and frequency in hearing from God. What must we do to increase our accuracy? Make a written plan and work with other believers who will hold you accountable. Journal your journey!

_____

_____

_____

_____

2. Right now, let's all once again re-commit again to the daily, meaningful, prayerful, "hungry" study of God's Word the Bible… always first for ourselves, then for others *(see section 8.1.3 Summary).*

9

God's 10 Conditions for Healing

Here are our learning objectives for Lesson 9:

- **Understand God's 10 Conditions for miraculous healing.**
- **How to meaningfully help those individuals who are not healed.**

Before we start, here are two important "disclaimers" for today's lesson. This chapter is primarily intended for ministry-minded believers who:

- …. Want God to use them to heal *others*. Be aware that much of this chapter is unnecessary for those whose only goal is to *receive* healing for themselves.

- …want to consistently heal mature, long-time Christians. This lesson is unnecessary for those wanting to heal new Christians or Hindus, Muslims, new Agers, Atheists and Agnostics.

_____

_____

_____

_____

_____

_____

9.1 God's 10 Conditions for Healing

Let us preform a careful review of God's ten conditions[25] which when met enable Him to act miraculously on our behalf in response to our requests… provided <u>none</u> of Satan's ten blocks are in place (to be studied in next week's lesson).

We will examine God's 10 conditions for healing one-by-one.

9.1.1 With Right Motives in Our Hearts

As with everything else we do, our inner motivations for wanting to heal the sick —or for that matter to be healed—truly matter to God:

- James 4:2b – 3 NLT:
  2b …yet you don't have what you want because you don't ask God for it. 3 And even when you ask, **you don't get it because your motives are all wrong**—you want only what will give you pleasure.

It is possible to want to heal or desire healing for the wrong reason(s). As examples, the desire to attract attention or "message sending" to others are sinful reasons.

9.1.2 According to God's Will

Our prayer requests for others or ourselves must align with God's Will:

- 1 John 5:14, 15 NIV:
  4 This is the confidence we have in approaching God: that if we ask anything according to his will, he hears us.
  15 And if we know that he hears us—whatever we ask—we know that we have what we asked of him.

This helps to explain why Jesus made this promise to us:

---

[25] This material is adapted from "Lesson 20: God's Ten Conditions for His Miraculous Response to Our Prayers" from *Expect to be Believe: 90 Bible Devotionals to Increase Your Faith for the Impossible"* by Paul Williams.

- John 14:13,14 NIV (Jesus):
  13 And I will do **whatever** you ask in my name, so that the Father may be glorified in the Son.
  14 You may ask me for **anything** in my name, and I will do it.

Our need to pray in alignment with the Will of God is yet another reason why our daily mediative study of God's Word is so vitally important. It should be extremely exciting to know that with sufficient time and effort we *can* indeed determine the perfect Will of God in every situation we encounter in life and ministry, as stated here:

- Romans 12:2 NIV:
  Do not conform to the pattern of this world but be transformed by the renewing of your mind. <u>**Then** **you will be able to test and approve what God's will is**</u>—His good, pleasing, and perfect will.

 Here is a big clue: God's promises in His Word the Bible *are* His perfect Will. For example, we know what the Will of God is about our physical healing of the sick and injured, because Jesus Himself told us:

- John 14:12 NIV (Jesus):
  12 Very truly I tell you, whoever believes in me will do the works I have been doing, and they will do even greater things than these, because I am going to the Father.

For inspiration, start by looking at Jesus' healing miracles, then claim God's promises from His Word the Bible by declaring them out loud with your lips. Finally, *demonstrate* your faith by *acting* on God's promises.

_____

_____

_____

_____

<u>For the full video recorded testimony, see page 5</u>.

<u>Illustrative Testimony:</u> In May 2021, a terminally ill emaciated stage 4 cancer patient at MD Anderson Hospital in Houston with only weeks to live was instantly healed, but only after she first repented of doubting God's Will for her healing. She immediately warmed up and began to speak without difficulty, and the next morning a full body scan at MD Anderson showed no trace of the cancer she was riddled with previously.

9.1.3 In Faith Derived from Hearing the Word of God

- Romans 10:17 NLT:
  So faith comes from hearing, that is, hearing the Good News about Christ.

In everything Jesus is our example and our patten. *"If Jesus did it, I can do it!"* (see again John 14:12). Our faith must be built upon Jesus' life and His example in the Word of God, not on someone's preaching or teaching or YouTube videos or this class… or on our feelings and whims of the day.

_____

_____

_____

_____

9.1.4 If We Remain in Jesus and His Words Remain in Us

A daily submitted, *living* connection with Jesus as our Lord and Savior through the Holy Spirit is an essential requirement for mature Christians to be healed:

- John 15:7 NLT (Jesus)):
  But **if you remain in Me <u>and</u> My words remain in you**, you may ask for anything you want, and **it will be granted!**

An *intellectual* experience with Jesus Christ is woefully insufficient. Your class instructors have noticed over the years that a disturbing number of long-time senior Christians as well as senior church leadership are intellectually living off *past* intimacy with the person of Jesus and the Holy Spirit. Their emotion-suppressed, stale experience with Jesus makes it all but impossible for them to be healed.

We know for a fac that Jesus is not pleased when we allow the fervor and intensity of our love for Him to wither away, because He clearly says so here:

- Revelation 2:4-6 NIV (Jesus):
  4 Yet I hold this against you: **You have forsaken the love you had at first.**
  5 Consider how far you have fallen! **Repent and do the things you did at first.** If you do not repent, I will come to you and remove your lampstand from its place.

Interestingly enough, when senior Christians and senior church leadership pursue and find their first love of Jesus again, as a by-product their long-suppressed, muted emotions of love and joy for Jesus begin to freely and radiantly overflowing again. Their faith becomes fresh, living, and strong, and their physical healing then becomes easy.

9.1.5 Without Harboring Known Sin in Our Hearts

Our obedience to Jesus and His commands is a necessity:

- 1 John 3:22 NLT:
  And we will receive from Him whatever we ask because we obey Him and do the things that please Him.

- Matthew 15:7-9 NLT:
  7 You hypocrites! Isaiah was right when he prophesied about you, for he wrotc,
  8 '**These people honor me with their lips, but their hearts are far from me.**
  9 Their worship is a farce, for they teach man-made ideas as commands from God.'

Our acts of obedience are not "working for our salvation," but rather are showing Jesus that we genuinely love Him in the way that He asks us to:

- John 14:15 NIV (Jesus):
  If you love me, tell me so and give me a great big hug.

Huh??? Whoops! Strange misprint there. Let's try this again:

- John 14:15 NIV (Jesus):
  If you love me, keep my commands.

_____

_____

_____

_____

9.1.6 Being Considerate and Respecting Our Spouses

We must be considerate and respectful of our spouses so that our prayers to God will not be hindered by our neglect and disrespect:

- 1 Pet. 3:7 NLT:
  In the same way, you husbands **must** give honor to your wives. Treat your wife **with understanding** as you live together. She may be weaker than you are, but she is your equal partner in God's gift of new life. **Treat her as you should so your prayers will not be hindered.**

While the prior scripture passage exhorts only men to treat their wives correctly, here are two related scripture passages which should be considered as well:

- Galatians 3:26-29 NIV:
  26 So in Christ Jesus you are all children of God through faith, 27 for all of you who were baptized into Christ have clothed yourselves with Christ.
  28 There is neither Jew nor Gentile, neither slave nor free, **nor is there male and female, for you are all one in Christ Jesus.**

29 If you belong to Christ, then you are Abraham's seed, and heirs according to the promise.

- Matthew 7:12 NIV (Jesus):
  So in everything, d**o to others what you would have them do to you**, for this sums up the Law and the Prophets.

_____

_____

_____

_____

9.1.7 While Bearing Fruit for God's Kingdom

We are here to bear fruit for God's Kingdom! God will prune us (ouch!) to lovingly encourage us to reproduce ourselves spiritually. If we still will not do so, then in time we will be cut off by the Father:

- John 15:16 NLT (Jesus):
  You didn't choose Me. I chose you. I appointed you to go and produce <u>lasting</u> fruit, so that the Father will give you whatever you ask for, using My Name.

- John 15:1-2 NIV (Jesus):
  1 I am the true vine, and my Father is the gardener.
  2 **He cuts off every branch in me that bears no fruit**, while every branch that does bear fruit, he prunes so that it will be even more fruitful.

- Matthew 25:14-30 NIV (read this full parable by Jesus in your own time in your Bibles):
    […]
  24 Then the man who had received one bag of gold came. 'Master,' he said, 'I knew that you are a hard man, harvesting where you have not sown and gathering where you have not scattered seed.
  25 So I was afraid and went out and hid your gold in the ground. See, here is what belongs to you.'

26 His master replied, **'You wicked, lazy servant!** So you knew that I harvest where I have not sown and gather where I have not scattered seed?
27 Well then, you should have put my money on deposit with the bankers, so that when I returned I would have received it back with interest.
28 **'So take the bag of gold from him** and give it to the one who has ten bags.
29 For whoever has will be given more, and they will have an abundance. **Whoever does not have, even what they have will be taken from them.**
30 And throw that **worthless servant outside, into the darkness, where there will be weeping and gnashing of teeth.'**

_____

_____

_____

_____

9.1.8 In Agreement with Another Believer

God loves unity among His children!

- Matthew 18:19 NLT:
  I also tell you this: **If two of you agree** here on earth concerning anything you ask, my Father in heaven **will do it for you.**

In practical reality, such agreement is often with the person who you are praying for or who is praying for you.

The Bible hints in several places about the enhanced victory that occurs when two or more Christians work in harmony together. Interestingly enough, the same effect occurs in reverse if we live in deliberate disobedience long enough:

- Deuteronomy 32:29-31 NIV:
  30 How could one man chase a thousand,
     or two put ten thousand to flight,
  unless their Rock had sold them,
     unless the Lord had given them up?
  31 For their rock is not like our Rock,
     as even our enemies concede.

_____

_____

_____

_____

9.1.9 Proclaiming Our Faith with Our Lips

It takes much more faith to speak our belief out loud to others than it does to quietly think or whisper to ourselves.

- Heb. 4:16 NLT:
  So let us come **boldly** to the throne of our gracious God. There we will receive his mercy, and we will find grace to help us when we need it most.

- 2 Cor. 4:13 NLT:
  But we continue to preach because we have the same kind of faith the psalmist had when he said, **'I believed in God, so I spoke.'**

What we say out loud with our lips makes every difference as to what happens to us and those we pray for:

- Matthew 9:28-30a NIV (Jesus to two blind men who said they believed He could heal them):
  29 Then he touched their eyes and said, **'According to your faith let it be done to you'**
  30 and their sight was restored.

- Romans 10:9,10 NIV:
  9 If you **declare with your mouth**, "Jesus is Lord," and believe in your heart that God raised him from the dead, you will be saved.
  10 For it is with your heart that you believe and are justified, and **it is with your mouth** that you profess your faith and are saved.

_____

_____

_____

9.1.10 Putting Our Faith into Action

According to God's Word, we must believe that we have received our miracle *before* we receive it… and then *demonstrate* our "belief" with *action*, not *feelings*:

- Mark 11:24 NLT (Jesus):
  I tell you, you can pray for anything, **and if you believe that you've** received it, it will be yours.

- James 2:14-26 NLT:
  So you see, **faith by itself isn't enough**. Unless it produces good deeds, it is dead and useless.

- 2 Cor. 5:7 NLT:
  For we live by believing **and not by seeing**.

- Acts 3:6-7 NLT:
  6 But Peter said, 'I don't have any silver or gold for you. But I'll give you what I have. In the name of Jesus Christ the Nazarene, get up and walk!'
  7 Then Peter took the lame man by the right hand and helped him up. **And as he did,** the man's feet and ankles were instantly healed and strengthened."

9.1.11 Summary of God's 10 Conditions

Does the prior list of God's ten conditions for healing seem to you like a lot of hoops to jump through? If so, think again. Recall the many pages of "fine print" terms you must sign to purchase the car you drive or the home you live in. It is interesting that, for these earthly treasures, we are willing to do whatever is necessary to get what we need.

Likewise, we must be willing to do whatever is necessary to gain heavenly treasure and our health as well.

In fact, let us go even further. Learn to think of God's ten conditions as merely being the submitted life under God and His Holy Spirit that we, as Christian believers, should have been living all along. When equipped with this mindset, God's terms for healing will not seem like burdensome conditions at all, but rather as a description of the normal Christian life as Jesus lived it.

For some of us, this may be a whole new way of looking at this. Meditate and pray about this as you continue to study God's Word. We pray you will decide to take your walk with God to new heights. All things are possible for those who earnestly seek God with all their heart, mind, and soul![26]

9.1.12 How to Help Individuals Who are Not Healed

God is faithful and reliable to heal in accordance with His promises in His Word the Bible, *unless* one of His ten conditions for healing are unmet... or one of Satan's ten blocks are in place (next chapter).

From this lesson and the following chapter it can be understood that whenever someone is not immediately healed, there is a tangible reason for it that can be discerned and thankfully corrected.

Never leave an unhealed person in a state of confusion in which they can fall into depression and/or fall prey to Satan's accusations against God and His Word. Always take the time to lovingly identify the problem(s) and either assist them in correcting them on the spot so they can be immediately healed, or if they are unwilling, to provide your contact information so they can follow up with you later as you continue praying and the Holy Spirit works in their life.

Tip: as a "Bible faith healer," it is helpful to carry your contact information with you in business card format so you can quickly pass out your card in any limited time situation, such as when doing street ministry or witnessing in a store or mall, etc.

---

[26] This summary was excerpted from "Expect To Believe: 90 Bible Devotionals to Increase Your Faith for the Impossible"

Additional Class Notes (Lesson Nine)

Your Personal Notes, Observations, and Class Activities

_____

_____

_____

_____

_____

_____

_____

_____

_____

_____

_____

_____

_____

_____

_____

_____

_____

_____

_____

_____

_____

Questions for the Instructors or the class:

1. _____

_____

_____

_____

_____

2. _____

_____

_____

_____

_____

3. _____

_____

_____

_____

_____

_____

9.2 Walking It Out – Class Assignment (LESSON NINE)

WALKING IT OUT Class Assignment (LESSON NINE)

OUR ACTION PLAN

<u>*Seek* JESUS</u> at a *<u>level and depth that you may not have previously</u>* to continually further develop and deepen your intimate, personal relationship with Jesus.

Continued Class Action Assignments

Read Daily: "Expect to Believe: 90 Bible Devotionals to Increase Your Faith for the Impossible" by Paul Williams (expect a close encounter with the Holy Spirit to happen while reading these devotionals daily).

Watch / Listen to the Class Lesson Videos; pause when needed to read-pray scriptures, work Action Plan steps, work Homework Challenges and Go Deeper **as** you go through your class notes AGAIN. (*Journaling revelations Holy Spirit has shown you*)

Review Weekly: Key Learning Objectives (*check off each one as you achieve the objectives of this week's lesson (see this chapter's Introduction). Ask the Holy Spirit to plant these objectives deep in your heart and mind and help put them into practice in your daily life.*)

Suggested Action: fast, creating an intimate relationship with God: (*per section 1.2 apply the three key takeaways that Paul learned*) God responds to fasting and prayer. *<u>Adding a Biblically based food-fast is even better and can aid in combination with God's Word and prayer to a significant breakthrough</u>* (see section 1.12) <u>**Speak aloud** the action items in the seven steps taken from James 4:7-10</u> (*especially steps 5& 6 (see section 1.12)*)

Daily abide in the overflow of the anointing of Holy Spirit (*as described in sections 1.5 and 1.6*). Ask the Holy Spirit **every day** to **soften your heart and fill you with God's amazing love** for Your fellow created human beings. Re-commit to earnestly seeking the Holy Ghost in His fullness in your life.

Daily read and apply the books of _John, Acts, and Ephesians_[27] *(see section 3.12)* using the "read-pray the Word approach" and the "Seven Steps to Intimate Relationship with God."

Always follow the lead of the Holy Spirit! His directions should always displace every plan and course of action of our own.

For a primer or refresher about the Holy Spirit, read-pray the scripture-packed overview in **Appendix A**, "Introduction to the Holy Spirit" *(journal what is revealed by the Holy Spirit)*.

Re-Read Study and Pray *chapters 6 and 7 "**Gifts of the Holy Spirit**,"* Parts 1 and 2.

Learn and commit to memory the practical limits of our authority in Christ to cast out demons and to heal the sick and injured. *(see section 5.5)*

Miracle working factors: *"When we believers speak God's Word boldly with our lips in the name of Jesus through the Holy Spirit's power indwelling within us, the result is signs, wonders, and miracles for the glory of God."*

Important: Speaking *forcefully* and/or *loudly* is neither important nor helpful in working a miracle, however, **speaking** *boldly* **always is (***whether in a loud or quiet voice***). This is because speaking** *forcefully* **typically is a manifestation of our** *emotions***, whereas speaking with** *boldness* **is a manifestation our** *faith.*

Eagerly desire the greater gifts of the Holy Spirit *(We must treasure, use, and grow these gifts)*

Do not guide your life by personal prophecies. *The Word and the Spirit always agree.* Never accept a personal prophecy from anyone without first confirming every portion of it directly yourself with the Word of God and the Holy Spirit, in that order. *(see section 6.4.1)*

As followers of Jesus, we all must make sure that our attention is not excessively focused on the flashy nine (9) Gifts of the Holy Spirit in 1 Corinthians 12:7-11 to the overlooking of the all-important, foundational nine (9) Fruits of the Holy Spirit in Galatians 5:22-23

---

[27] In our observation, no other combination of three books in the Bible gives as much spiritual return for the time expended. These three books serve as an effective jumping point to real-pray the remainder of the entire Bible.

Honestly ask yourself if each of the Fruits of the Holy Spirit are displayed in your life in ever-increasing measure… and if not, prayerfully ask the Holy Spirit as to why not and what is the appropriate corrective remedy.

Take the self-examination questionnaire *(see section 8.1.2)* and make it a regular part of your lifestyle. *Refer back to it frequently.*

Pray to the Holy Spirit for instruction and guidance to develop" The Knowing".

From an earlier lesson's homework assignment, use the same exhortation for this coming week:

> **Ephesians 6:18 NIV:**
> 18 **And pray in the Spirit on all occasions** with all kinds of prayers and requests. With this in mind, be alert and always keep on praying for all the Lord's people.

Action Assignments for Lesson Nine →

Learn to think of God's ten conditions as merely being the submitted life under God and His Holy Spirit that we, as Christian believers, should have been living all along.

HOMEWORK CHALLENGE

1. If our internal motivations for wanting to heal others are not pleasing to God, what can happen?

_____

_____

_____

_____

2. How can we know whether our motivations are good ones or not?

_____

_____

_____

_____

_____

3. Is there a difference between faith that results from hearing others teach on the subject and faith that results directly from our personal and prayerful study of God's Word?

_____

_____

_____

_____

_____

4. How important is it that the teachings and words of Jesus remain vivid and fresh on our minds and in our hearts? What are two things that can happen if the teaching and words of Jesus slip in their clarity in our minds?

_____

_____

_____

_____

_____

_____

5. Does it matter if we are consistently kind, considerate, understanding, and loving to everyone except our spouse? Why?

_____

_____

_____

_____

_____

6. Jesus told us to heal the sick. So if I am healing the sick, does it really matter whether I am bringing souls to Jesus or not?

_____

_____

_____

_____

_____

7. What are two ways that a fellow believer can assist you when you pray for healing of the sick?

_____

_____

_____

_____

_____

_____

8. Why is it important for a Christian believer whom you just prayed for to demonstrate their faith for their healing by their actions?

_____

_____

_____

_____

_____

GOING DEEPER (Journal Time)

1. How can we be certain beyond any doubt whatsoever that it is <u>always</u> God's will to heal <u>everyone</u> who is sick or injured? If we are unable to reach this level of certainty, what is likely to happen?

_____

_____

2. Based on everything you have learned in this class from the beginning to now, what are two ways can we tell if sin in our life is in danger of undermining the effectiveness of our witness and prayers for others?

_____

_____

3. What was your definition of Godly faith prior to this class? What is your definition of Godly faith now?

_____

_____

_____

4. SCENARIO: You are praying for a Christian believer who has an ankle which healed years ago from a compound bone fracture suffered in an accident. However, the medical profession installed metal screws and pins inside the ankle to hold it together so it could heal, leaving it unable to bend. After your prayer for healing, this believer attempts to walk normally on their ankle to demonstrate their faith to God for their healing. However, every time he or she tries to do so, the metal screws and pins prevent the ankle from bending. So this believer tells you that he or she is waiting for God to remove the metal screws and pins first so he or she can then walk on it. What should you say and do to help this Christian believer past this seemingly unsolvable dilemma so he or she can be healed on the spot by God?

_____

_____

_____

_____

10

Satan's 10 Blocks to Healing

HERE ARE OUR LEARNING objectives for this final Lesson 10:

- Understanding Satan's 10 Blocks to Healing.
- Our need for reserve oil – the "over-abundance" of the Holy Spirit.
- Class Completion Certificates & Celebration time!
- Student testimonies and prayer for each other (as time allows)

10.1 Overcoming Our Determined Enemy

We will study our enemy's 10 blocks to God's healing power one-by-one. Our goal is learning how to identify, defeat and remove these obstacles. The 10 Satanic blocks are arranged in this chapter with the most frequently encountered blocks appearing first, as observed in our experience.

10.1.1 Unforgiveness Toward Others, God, or Even Ourselves (#1)

If we will not forgive others who have hurt or wronged us, not only will God not heal us, but far worst yet we will place ourselves in serious risk of not being saved either, as stated here:

- Matthew 6:14 (Jesus):

  14 For if you forgive other people when they sin against you, your heavenly Father will also forgive you.

  15 **But if you do not forgive others their sins, your Father will not forgive your sins.**

- Mark 11:24,25 NIV (Jesus):

  24 I tell you, you can pray for anything, and if you believe that you've received it, it will be yours.

  25 But when you are praying, **first forgive anyone you are holding a grudge against, so that your Father in heaven will forgive your sins, too.**

The key operative term here is *"forgive,"* not *"forget."* Many Christians say they are not holding grudges against anyone, when in reality, all that has happened is they have decided to <u>forget</u> about what happened and move on.

Stubborn unforgiveness forms a block to healing. Unforgiveness can only be removed when a conscious decision is made to forgive those who have hurt us. Then, we must release all our charges and expectations from those we have forgiven.

Important: forgive God and yourself as applicable. In all cases speak boldly aloud with your lips.

_____

_____

_____

_____

10.1.2 Unworthiness Before God (#2)

Some Christians do not feel worthy before God and therefore are hesitant to ask for their healing or receive healing prayer from others. Often it requires discernment from the Holy Spirit to detect this problem exists, since those feel unworthy may not show it on the outside or may even deny it is an issue if asked.

Thankfully, all Chrisian believers are worthy of God's healing blessings simply because the death, burial and resurrection of His Son Jesus makes us worthy. Here is a reminder from scripture of our worthiness before God (re-review section 2.3.1, *"Foundational Truth #1 of 3: Who Am I in Christ?"* **as** may be **necessary)**:

- Hebrew 4:14-16 NIV:

  14 Therefore, since we have a great high priest who has ascended into heaven, Jesus the Son of God, let us hold firmly to the faith we profess.

  15 For we do not have a high priest who is unable to empathize with our weaknesses, but we have one who has been tempted in every way, just as we are—yet he did not sin.

  16 Let us then approach God's throne of grace **with confidence**, so that we may receive mercy and find grace to help us in our time of need. [NLT translation: "**come boldly**"]

- John 17:22-23 NLT (Jesus):

  22 I have given them the glory you gave me, so they may be one as we are one.

  23 I am in them and you are in me. May they experience such perfect unity that the world will know that you sent me and **that you love them as much as you love me.**

10.1.3 Unsure of God's Will for Your Healing (#3)

Faith is not believing that God *can* heal you. Rather, it is believing that God *will* heal you.

Many Christians are quick to say, "I believe God can do anything. I *know* He can heal me *if* He wants to!" This "if" type of "faith" in what God "can" do does not result in miraculous healing. To counter this thinking, here are seven different examples where Jesus healed **everyone** who came to Him plus additionally an account of Jesus' disciples likewise doing the same:

- Matthew 8:16 NLT:

  That evening many demon-possessed people were brought to Jesus. He cast out the evil spirits with a simple command, and **he healed all the sick**.

- Math 12:15 NIV:

  Aware of this, Jesus withdrew from that place. A large crowd followed him, and **he healed all who were ill**.

- Matthew 15:29-31 NLT:

  29 Jesus returned to the Sea of Galilee and climbed a hill and sat down.

  30 A vast crowd brought to him people who were lame, blind, crippled, those who couldn't speak, and many others. They laid them before Jesus, and **he healed them all.**

31 The crowd was amazed! Those who hadn't been able to speak were talking, the crippled were made well, the lame were walking, and the blind could see again! And they praised the God of Israel.

- Mark 6:56 NLT:
  Wherever he went—in villages, cities, or the countryside—they brought the sick out to the marketplaces. They begged him to let the sick touch at least the fringe of his robe, and **all who touched him were healed**.

- Luke 4:40 NLT:
  As the sun went down that evening, people throughout the village brought sick family members to Jesus. No matter what their diseases were, the touch of his hand **healed everyone**.

- Luke 6:19 NLT:
  Everyone tried to touch him, because healing power went out from him, and **he healed everyone**.

- Luke 9:1 NLT:
  One day Jesus called together his twelve disciples and gave them power and authority to **cast out all demons** and to **heal all diseases**.

- Acts 5:16 NIV (Peter):
  Crowds gathered also from the towns around Jerusalem, bringing their sick and those tormented by impure spirits, and **all of them were heal**ed.

- 1 Peter 2:24 NLT:
  24 He personally **carried our sins**
    in his body on the cross
  so that we can be dead to sin
     and live for what is right.
  By his wounds **you are healed**.

Notice that this scripture does not say, "Jesus carried *most* of our sins on the cross, and by His wounds *most* of you are healed." Rather, Jesus' sacrifice paid the price for *all* of our sins <u>and</u> *all* of our sicknesses, as eloquently stated here:

- Psalms 103:2, 3 NIV:
  Praise the Lord, my soul,
      and forget not all his benefits—
  3 who forgives **all** your sins
      and heals **all** your diseases.

Question: okay then, Jesus the Son of God healed everyone, got it. However, what about us? How do we know that *we* can heal everyone?

Answer: John 14:12 NLT (Jesus): I tell you the truth, anyone who believes in me will do the same works I have done, and even greater works, because I am going to be with the Father.

All right everyone, it is time to repeat our class motto from Lesson 2:

"If Jesus did it, I can do it!"

Amen hallelujah!

_____

_____   _____   _____

_____

_____

10.1.4 Unbelief / Lack of Faith (#4)

We must have faith in God and His Word to successfully ask Him for anything:

- Hebrews 11:6 NLT:
  And it is impossible to please God without faith. Anyone who wants to come to him must believe that God exists and that he rewards those who sincerely seek him.

Accordingly, our enemy will try everything in his power to steal or impede our faith. One of his key tactics is to attempt to divert our attention away from God's Word and His promises to our natural circumstances (what we see, feel, hear, or even need).

Let us examine how the people of Jesus' hometown of Nazareth were derailed in their faith. They could not look past what they saw and thought they knew ("man's facts"), when instead they should have kept their attention focused solely and only on what the Old Testament scriptures had to say about the birth, upbringing, and life of Jesus ("God's truth"):

- Mark 6:1-6 NLT:
  6 Jesus left that part of the country and returned with his disciples to Nazareth, his hometown.
  2 The next Sabbath he began teaching in the synagogue, and many who heard him were amazed. They asked, 'Where did he get all this wisdom and the power to perform such miracles?'
  3 Then they scoffed, 'He's just a carpenter, the son of Mary and the brother of James, Joseph, Judas, and Simon. And his sisters live right here among us.' They were deeply offended **and refused to believe in him.**
  4 Then Jesus told them, 'A prophet is honored everywhere except in his own hometown and among his relatives and his own family.'
  5 And because of their unbelief, he couldn't do any miracles among them except to place his hands on a few sick people and heal them.
  6 And he was amazed at their unbelief.

- 2 Corinthians 5:7 NIV:
  For we live by faith, **not by sight**. [NLT: For we live by believing and **not by seeing.**]

_____

_____

_____

_____

God's *truth* beats man's "*facts*" every time…. provided we keep our minds focused on what God's Word says, rather than on our circumstances or what we see, hear, feel, and "know" to be factual.

10.1.5 Surface Knowledge of God's Word (#5)

We have often noticed that it may require several hours to heal Christians who have only a surface knowledge of God's Word instead of a deep inner spirit/soul acceptance[28].

As a review of what we learned in Chapter 3, we should remember:

- Satan quoted scripture to Jesus.

- Some atheists study God's Word and may quote it accurately, although typically incompletely.

Clearly knowledge of the scriptures alone is insufficient. What is missing in both cases above is the *saving knowledge* of Jesus Christ and the *anointing and Presence* of the Holy Spirit.

It is the anointing of the Holy Spirit that breaks the yokes of oppression and physical bondage:

- Acts 10:38 NLT:
  …God anointed Jesus of **Nazareth with the Holy Spirit and with power**. <u>Then</u> Jesus went around doing good and healing all who were oppressed by the devil, **for God was with him.**

_____

_____

_____

_____

10.1.6 Unconfessed Sin (#6)

Note: inspiration for this portion of this lesson has been drawn from *"Barriers to Healing"* by deceased world-renown Bible teacher and noted healing evangelist Derek Prince[29].

---

[28] Noted deceased international healing evangelist Derek Prince names "ignorance of God's Word" as his top number reason why the sick is not healed.

[29] *"Barriers to Healing"* https://youtu.be/MFOPC6gsFec

There is no record in the Bible of Jesus our example ever asking anyone to repent of sin, believe in Him, or change even the smallest detail about their lives prior to Jesus healing them.

We do, however, have one example of how Jesus healing a paralyzed man first before then telling him *afterwards* to stop sinning:

- John 5:14 NIV:
Later Jesus found (an invalid man He had just healed) at the temple and said to him, 'See, you are well again. **Stop sinning or something worse may happen to you.'**

Nevertheless, from a study of scriptures passages by Jesus apostles it does appear that sin in those needing healing may prevent some of them from receiving their healings:

- James 5:16 NLT:
Confess your sins to each other and pray for each **other so that you may be healed.** The earnest prayer of a righteous person has great power and produces wonderful results.

- Proverbs 28:13 NLT:
People who conceal their sins **will not prosper**, but if they confess and turn from them, **they will receive mercy**.

- Hebrews 3:12, 13 NLT:
12 Be careful then, dear brothers and sisters. Make sure that your own hearts are not evil and unbelieving, **turning you away from the living God.**
13 You must warn each other every day, while it is still 'today,' so that none of you will be deceived by sin and **hardened against God.**

Additionally, unconfessed sin in the life of the believer who is doing the healing can indeed block his or her prayers on behalf of the person who needs healing. This is implied, although not explicitly stated, in the following pair of scripture passages:

- 1 John 3:22 NLT:
And we will receive from Him **whatever we ask** because we obey Him and do the things that please Him.

- John 14:15 NIV (Jesus):
If you love me, **keep my commands.**

Here is a testimony of how unconfessed sin in the life of a famous Bible healer blocked his prayers for the healing of his own son. The following testimony is excerpted from *"The Collected Works of John G. Lake"* by renown Bible healer John G. Lake (1870 – 1935), who famously healed over 100,000 people in the Spokane, Washington area in the span of just five short years:

"One of my sons was dying with pneumonia once. I prayed for that fellow and I prayed for him, and it was not a bit of good. But one day I was downtown, and I was praying about that boy and the Lord said, 'You go home and confess your sins to your wife.'

And I said, 'I will.' I stopped and got one of the old elders to come down to my house. As we rode along, we talked together, and I said, 'I have some things I want to fix up with my wife before you pray. There have been all kinds of prayer, but He will not hear.'

So, I took my wife to the other room and told her the whole business, all there was, and we went into the other room and prayed for that son and he was healed in a second.

I want to tell you that when Christians are not healed, as a rule you get digging around and get the Holy Ghost to help you, and when they have vomited out all the stuff, they will get the healing."

10.1.7 Occult Involvement (#7)

Even a periphery of involvement with the occult in your past or present that remains unrepented of may be a block to physical healing.

Surprisingly enough, involvement in the occult even includes two surprising sources:

- Substantial prior (or current!) enjoyment of and addiction to hard rock music.

- Use of illegal hallucinating drugs or abuse/overdose of hallucinating prescription drugs. Drug-induced hallucinations are frequently used by demons to force their thoughts and values into the innermost core of their victims in order to set up obstacles and contradictions to the operation of God's Word and the Holy Spirit in their lives.

> <u>For the full video recorded testimony, see page 5</u>.
>
> <u>Illustrative Testimony</u>: a man with hundreds of demonic hard rock CDs in his home decided (with some compelling persuasion!) to clean up his home and throw his CD collection away… except for a single CD that he deliberately left behind hidden in his bed's mattress covering. What could possibly be wrong with failing to discard a single hard rock CD? Watch this riveting testimony to find out!

10.1.8 Idolatry and False gods (#8)

We are commanded not to associate or make covenants with false gods. This includes all secret societies such as the Free Masons.

- Exodus 23:32 NLT:
  Make no treaties with them or their gods.

This instruction applies to both to such people and their gods.

10.1.9 Generational Curses On Your Family Line (#9)

Jesus was made a curse for us, so we can be free! If you or your family line have had past or current association of any kind with the occult and its practitioners or their possessions that has not been repented of, it's time. Such involvements should be thoroughly repented of with all occult related possessions burned or thrown away. Additionally, <u>all</u> learned "knowledge" from these sources should be repudiated (forsaken and disavowed).

- Exodus 34:7 NLT:
  I lavish unfailing love to a thousand generations. I forgive iniquity, rebellion, and sin. But I do not excuse the guilty. I lay the sins of the parents upon their children and grandchildren; **the entire family is affected— even children in the third and fourth generations.**

Here are 10 specific curses pronounced by God Himself that are listed in the Bible:

- Deuteronomy 27:14-26 NLT:

  15 Cursed is anyone who carves or casts an idol and secretly sets it up.

  16 Cursed is anyone who dishonors father or mother.

  17 Cursed is anyone who steals property from a neighbor by moving a boundary marker.

  18 Cursed is anyone who leads a blind person astray on the road.

  19 Cursed is anyone who denies justice to foreigners, orphans, or widows.

  20 Cursed is anyone who has sexual intercourse with one of his father's wives, for he has violated his father.

  21 Cursed is anyone who has sexual intercourse with an animal.

  22 Cursed is anyone who has sexual intercourse with his sister, whether she is the daughter of his father or his mother.

  23 Cursed is anyone who has sexual intercourse with his mother-in-law.

  24 Cursed is anyone who attacks a neighbor in secret.

  25 Cursed is anyone who accepts payment to kill an innocent person.

  26 Cursed is anyone who does not affirm and obey the terms of these instructions.

Additionally, be aware that we can actually impose curses on ourselves in the form of ill-advised words, referred to as ungodly vows (examples: *"I will never trust anyone to treat me right (or care for me, etc.)"* or even (gasp!) *"I will never trust God to tell me what to do without me first knowing why."*

 Caution: a full set of teaching on the topic of breaking generational curses and ungodly vows is extensive and quite involved. For this reason, this topic is best covered in separate dedicated class(es) which this ministry offers as well as supports through other ministries.

10.1.10 Unscriptural Covenants With the Enemies of God (#10)

Judgement of an entire nation or a group of people can occur as the result of a broken national covenant or unscriptural national covenant. Both the innocent and guilty in such a nation or people group may all suffer alike.

An eye-opening example of this in the Bible is the story of the Gibeonites:

- Summary: In Joshua chapter 9, the Gibeonites deceived Israel into making an ungodly treaty covenant with them. Then many decades later in 2 Samuel chapter 21, God punished the nation of Israel with a 3-year long famine because years earlier King Saul had broken his nation's (ungodly!) covenant with the Gibeonites. When king David avenged the Gibeonites for their losses, God ended the famine.

A modern-day example:

A demonic "Zero-Year Curse" by American Indian "prophet" Tenskwatawa resulted in the assassination death or assassination attempt on the life of every U.S. President who took office every 20 years apart from 1860–1980, a stretch of 120 straight years without letup. This curse was broken by intercessory prayer after an assassination attempt on U.S. President Ronald Reagan, who was elected in 1980.

10.2 Overflowing Abundance of the Holy Spirit

With Satan's 10 blocks to God's healing power now out of the way, it is time to conclude this 10-week Bible Study series with a final exhortation once again to seek the Holy Spirit and the *fullness* of His power.

Our need for an overflowing abundance of the Holy Spirit can be clearly seen from Jesus' parable of the Five Wise and Five Foolish Virgins:

- Matthew 25:1-13 NIV (Jesus):
  1. At that time the kingdom of heaven will be like ten virgins who took their lamps and went out to meet the bridegroom.
  2 Five of them were foolish and five were wise.
  3 The foolish ones took their lamps but did not take any oil with them.
  4 The wise ones, however, took oil in jars along with their lamps.
  5 The bridegroom was a long time in coming, **and they all became drowsy and fell asleep.**
  6 At midnight the cry rang out: 'Here is the bridegroom! Come out to meet him!'
  7 Then all the virgins woke up and trimmed their lamps.
  8 The foolish ones said to the wise, 'Give us some of your oil; our lamps are going out.'

9 'No,' they replied, 'there may not be enough for both us and you. Instead, go to those who sell oil and buy some for yourselves.'

10 But while they were on their way to buy the oil, the bridegroom arrived. The virgins who were ready went in with him to the wedding banquet. And the door was shut.

11 Later the others also came. 'Lord, Lord,' they said, 'open the door for us!'

12 But he replied, 'Truly I tell you, I don't know you.'

13 Therefore keep watch, because you do not know the day or the hour.

We can see in this parable our need for a reserve "stockpile" of the Holy Spirit within us. This reserve "overflow" of the Holy Spirit will help us to outlast unexpected delays in receiving God's promises amid the stresses, problems, and temptations of everyday life.

As an additional benefit, our reserve overflow stockpile of the Holy Spirit will allow God to work signs, wonders, and miracles through us for ourselves and others even when we are worn out, tired and weary.

Jesus Himself provides us with the best possible example of this reserve of the Holy Spirit within Him:

- Matthew 14:1-21 NIV:
  (Background from verses 1-11: Jesus' cousin John the Baptist had just been beheaded in prison by Herod)
  12 John's disciples came and took (John's body minus his head) and buried it. **Then they went and told Jesus.**
  13 When Jesus heard what had happened, **he withdrew by boat privately to a solitary place.** Hearing of this, the crowds followed him on foot from the towns.
  14 When Jesus landed and saw a large crowd, **he had compassion on them and healed their sick.**
  (Summary of verses 15-21: Jesus feeds about 20,000 people, described as "about five thousand men, besides women and children")

Notice how during one of Jesus' lowest personal moments of his earthly humanity, he did not become frustrated, upset, irritable, or take a time-out break for Himself. Instead, His abundant reserve oil of the Holy Spirit allowed him to still feel the compassion of His heavenly Father for the people and perform one of the greatest miracles of His earthly ministry.

Summary: Jesus took the time required to build and maintain a close, intimate relationship with the person of the Holy Spirit. So, it should be with each of us. Thank you, Jesus, for your amazing example as a human being just like us 2,000 years ago here on earth!

10.3 Two Radical Testimonies: Class Summary!

As you doubtlessly recall, this 10-week class series is entitled in full, *"Extreme Faith for Extreme Evangelism™, Physical Healing, Prophecy, and more."* This point and purpose of this class is demonstrated in full by the following two final radical testimonies.

 <u>For the full video recorded testimony, see page 5</u>.

<u>Testimony #1</u>: story of the April 7, 2022, drastic healing and salvation of a man and his family and their release from terror by demons. Case history highlights:

- Prophetic revelation from the Holy Spirit (2 sets)
- Remarkable on-the-spot physical healings
- Radical salvation by the husband, wife, and youngest daughter
- Permanent release from years of drug addiction
- Saving the life of an unborn child
- Casting out of demons from a possessed home
- …and the start of immediate Biblical discipleship.

Every aspect of Archie and his family's life changed for good on this date. This story in sum total is perhaps the ultimate example of all four goals of this class illustrated in a single testimony!

<u>Testimony #2</u>: This is a radical testimony from an unexpected place: a secular class being taught at a law enforcement facility. **This is a radical example of the power of the mighty Holy Spirit at work… and in** the most unanticipated of places, times, and ways at that. This is our final reminder once again that we are <u>totally dependent</u> on the Holy Spirit as the source of our miracle working power.

Here are highlights from this May 2015 powerful case history:

- 200 officials, law enforcement personnel, and agents were instantly struck down on the floor weeping by the overwhelming power of the Holy Spirit

- Public repentance, conviction, and salvation before all followed for about 40 people.

- This facility's official secular training agenda was held up for about two hours.

- **All of this occurred <u>WITHOUT</u> a message, altar call or invitation!!!**

This is our final reminder to seek God, His Kingdom, <u>and</u> His Righteousness, so all these things that we want (such as miracles) will be given to us:

- Matthew 6:33 NIV (Jesus):
  But seek first his kingdom and his righteousness, **and all these things will be given to you as well.**

All praise to our loving Father God and His Son Jesus. Hallelujah!

10.4 Student Testimonies and a Time of Prayer

{Applicable to our in-person classes only: time for student class testimonies, final questions/comments, and prayer for each other as the Holy Spirit so leads}

10.5 We are Done. Celebration Time!!!!

{Applicable to our in-person classes only: CELEBRATION & PRESENTATION OF CLASS COMPLETION CERTIFICATES TO ALL STUDENTS!!!}

Additional Class Notes (Lesson Ten)

Your Personal Notes, Observations, and Class Activities

Questions for the Instructors or the class:

1. _____

_____

_____

_____

_____

2. _____

_____

_____

_____

_____

3. _____

_____

_____

_____

_____

_____

10.6 Walking It Out – Class Assignment (LESSON TEN)!!!

WALKING IT OUT   Class Assignment (LESSON TEN)

OUR ACTION PLAN

Seek **JESUS** at a *level and depth that you may not have previously* to continually further develop and deepen your intimate, personal relationship with Jesus.

Class Action Assignments

Read Daily: "Expect to Believe: 90 Bible Devotionals to Increase Your Faith for the Impossible" by Paul Williams (expect a close encounter with the Holy Spirit to happen while reading these devotionals daily).

Watch / Listen to the Class Lesson Videos; pause when needed to read-pray scriptures, work Action Plan steps, work Homework Challenges and Go Deeper **as** you go through your class notes AGAIN. (*Journaling revelations Holy Spirit has shown you*)

Review Weekly: Key Learning Objectives (*check off each one as you achieve the objectives of this week's lesson (see this chapter's Introduction). Ask the Holy Spirit to plant these objectives deep in your heart and mind and help put them into practice in your daily life.*

Suggested Action: fast, creating an intimate relationship with God: (*per section 1.2 apply the three key takeaways that the author learned).* God responds to fasting and prayer. ***Adding a Biblically based food-fast is even better and can aid in combination with God's Word and prayer to a significant breakthrough*** (see section 1.12) ***Speak aloud** the action items in the seven steps taken from James 4:7-10* (*especially steps 5& 6 (see section 1.12)).*

Daily abide in the overflow of the anointing of Holy Spirit (*as described in sections 1.5 and 1.6).* Ask the Holy Spirit **every day** to **soften your heart and fill you with God's amazing love** for Your fellow created human beings. Re-commit to earnestly seeking the Holy Ghost in His fullness in your life..

Daily read and apply the books of _John, Acts, and Ephesians_[30] *(see section 1.12)* using the "read-pray the Word approach" and the "Seven Steps to Intimate Relationship with God."

Always follow the lead of the Holy Spirit! His directions must always immediately displace every plan and course of action of our own. Speak only what the Holy Spirit tells you to.

For a primer or refresher about the Holy Spirit, read-pray the scripture-packed overview in **Appendix A**, "Introduction to the Holy Spirit" *(journal what is revealed by the Holy Spirit)*.

Re-Read Study and Pray *chapters 6 and 7 "Gifts of the Holy Spirit,"* Parts 1 and 2.

Learn and commit to memory the practical limits of our authority in Christ to cast out demons and to heal the sick and injured. *(see section 5.5)*

Miracle working factors: *"When we believers speak God's Word boldly with our lips in the name of Jesus through the Holy Spirit's power indwelling within us, the result is signs, wonders, and miracles for the glory of God."*

Important: Speaking *forcefully* and/or *loudly* is neither important nor helpful in working a miracle, however, **speaking _boldly_ <u>always</u> is (***whether in a loud or quiet voice*). **This is because speaking** *forcefully* **typically is a manifestation of our** *emotions*, **whereas speaking with** *boldness* **is a manifestation our** *faith*.

Eagerly desire the greater **gifts of the Holy Spirit** *(You must treasure, use, and grow these gifts)*

Do not guide your life by personal prophecies. *The Word and the Spirit always agree.* Never accept a personal prophecy from anyone without first confirming it directly yourself with the Word of God and the Holy Spirit, in that order. *(see section 6.4.1)*

As followers of Jesus, we all must make sure that our attention is not excessively focused on the flashy nine (9) Gifts of the Holy Spirit in 1 Corinthians 12:7-11 to

---

[30] In our observation, no other combination of three books in the Bible gives as much spiritual return for the time expended. These three books serve as an effective jumping point to real-pray the remainder of the entire Bible.

the overlooking of the all-important, foundational nine (9) Fruits of the Holy Spirit in Galatians 5:22-23

Honestly ask yourself if each of the Fruits of the Holy Spirit are displayed in your life in ever-increasing measure… and if not, prayerfully ask the Holy Spirit as to why not and what is the appropriate corrective remedy

Take the self-examination questionnaire *(see section 8.1.2)* and make it a regular part of your lifestyle. *Refer back to it frequently.*

Pray to the Holy Spirit for instruction and guidance to develop" The Knowing".

Once again use this exhortation for this coming week:

> **Ephesians 6:18 NIV:**
> 18 **And pray in the Spirit on all occasions** with all kinds of prayers and requests. With this in mind, be alert and always keep on praying for all the Lord's people.

Learn to think of God's ten conditions as merely being the submitted life under God and His Holy Spirit that we, as Christian believers, should have been living all along.

Action Assignments for Lesson Ten →

Continue to seek the Holy Spirit and the *fullness* of His power. *We need an overflowing abundance of the Holy Spirit, a reserve stockpile for unexpected events.*

Remember to seek God, His Kingdom, <u>and</u> His Righteousness *so all these things that we want (**such as miracles**) will be given to us:*

> **Matthew 6:33 NIV (Jesus):**
> But **seek first his kingdom and his righteousness**, and all these things will be given to you as well.

HOMEWORK CHALLENGE

1. What would you say to a Christian believer who needs healing who tells you that he or she previously resented their father but then adds, "I'm past all that now… that was years ago."

_____

_____

_____

_____

_____

2. What would you say to someone who tells you, "I don't feel unworthy before God; however, I still don't want to bother Him with too many requests, either."?

_____

_____

_____

_____

_____

3. How would you respond to a believer who needs healing, who informs you, "I believe Jesus will heal me, unless I have Paul's 'thorn in the flesh' (Corinthians 12:6)."?

_____

_____

_____

_____

_____

4. How does Matthew 25:1-13 show our need for an overflowing abundance of the Holy Spirit?

_____

_____

_____

_____

5. As you read aloud through the scriptures in section 10.1.9, make a list of the ones you and/or your family either have now or had previously. Do some light research to note the many generational curses that can affect a family. Do you have or have knowledge of any of these curses in your family line? List them. Fast and pray to break these generational curses.

_____

_____

_____

_____

GOING DEEPER (Journal Time)

1. Is it good enough for a believer to forgive someone, without letting that person know that they have been forgiven (assuming that individual can and is willing to be contacted):

_____

_____

_____

_____

2. Scenario: A Christian believer friend of yours has attended a church that for decades has not believed in miraculous healing, so your friend for decades has believed likewise for decades. Your friend now has cancer and needs healing. So you show your friend several scriptures on the subject, who then firmly declares, "I now believe Jesus still heals today." You then pray for your friend's healing. Based upon this scenario and no other considerations, is your friend likely to be healed? Based upon what you learned in this final Lesson 10, why or why not?

_____

_____

3. Scenario: You and several believers who all have a confirmed gift of healing have all prayed separately and together for a friend who needs healing. However, the friend has not been healed. Upon further questioning, you discover that while your friend has never had anything to do with witchcraft, from early childhood her parents did. Does anything need to be done by you and/or your friend who needs healing? If so, what?

_____

_____

4. SCENARIO: You are praying for a Christian believer who has an ankle which healed years ago from multiple compound bone fractures suffered in an accident. However, the medical profession installed metal screws and pins inside the ankle to hold it together so it could heal. This believer wants to walk normally on their ankle to demonstrate their faith to God for their healing. However, every time he or she tries to do so, the metal screws and pins prevent the ankle from bending. So this believer tells you that he or she is waiting for God to remove the metal screws and pins so he or she can then walk on it.

What should you say and do to help this Christian believer move past this seemingly unsolvable dilemma so he or she can be healed on the spot by God?

_____

_____

5. Scenario: A close and dear believer friend of yours strongly believes and teaches that Biblical healing is for today. Your friend constantly studies scriptures in God's Word on this subject and prayerfully meditates on them. She knows the most important scripture passages by heart and is quick to quote them. Your friend furthermore strongly believes in the power in the name of Jesus, knows her authority in Christ, and how to use her authority. Yet your friend prays for the sick, healing seldom occurs… especially not in public away from church.

You notice that your friend seldom if ever makes any substantive references to the Holy Spirit. Based on everything that has been taught in this class from the beginning, in particular Lesson 1 and the end of this Lesson 10, what would you tell your friend and why?

Write your prayerful, well-thought-out answer here:

_____

_____

_____

_____

_____

_____

_____

_____

10.7 We are Done. Exercise Your Faith and Evangelize!!!!

Tell others about this class!!!

11

Appendix A: Introduction to the Holy Spirit

THIS APPENDIX IS COMPANION study material to Lesson 1. It is designed for those who may need a primer or a refresher on who the Holy Spirit is, what does He do, and what is His purpose.

11. The Holy Spirit is a Person

The Holy Spirit is a *Person* who makes decisions and can be sought for advice:

- 1 Cor. 12:11 NLT: "It is the one and only Spirit **who** distributes all these gifts. **He alone** decides which gift each person should have."

- Acts 13:2 NLT: "One day as these men were worshiping the Lord and fasting, **the Holy Spirit said**, 'Appoint Barnabas and Saul for the special work to which **I** have called them.'"

- Acts 13:4 NLT: So, Barnabas and Saul were **sent out by the Holy Spirit**. They went down to the seaport of Seleucia and then sailed for the island of Cyprus.

- Acts 15:28 For it seemed good **to the Holy Sp**irit and to us to lay no greater burden on you than these few requirements.

- Acts 20:22-23 NLT: And now I am bound **by the Spirit** to go to Jerusalem. I don't know what awaits me, except that the **Holy Spirit tells me** in city after city that jail and suffering lie ahead.

- Acts 5:3 NLT: Then Peter said, 'Ananias, why have you let Satan fill your heart? You **lied to the Holy Spirit**, and you kept some of the money for yourself.'

EXTREME FAITH *for* EXTREME EVANGELISM

The Holy Spirit is Our Teacher and Guide

- John 14:15-17 NLT (Jesus):

  15 If you love me, obey my commandments.

  16 And I will ask the Father, and he will give you another **Advocate**, who will never leave you.

  17 He is the Holy Spirit, **who leads into all truth**. The world cannot receive him because it isn't looking for him and doesn't recognize him. But you know him because he lives with you now and later **will be in you."**

- John 15:26 NLT (Jesus): But I will send you the **Advocate** —the **Spirit of truth**. He will come to you from the Father and will **testify all about me**.

- John 13:20 NLT (Jesus): I tell you the truth, **anyone who welcomes my messenger is welcoming me**, and anyone who welcomes me is welcoming the Father who sent me.

- John 16:5-15 NLT (Jesus):

  5 But now I am going away to the one who sent me, and not one of you is asking where I am going.

  6 Instead, you grieve because of what I've told you. |

  7 But in fact, **it is best for you that I go away, because if I don't, the Advocate won't come.** If I do go away, then I will send him to you.

  8 And when he comes, he will convict the world of its sin, and of God's righteousness, and of the coming judgment.

  9 The world's sin is that it refuses to believe in me.

  10 Righteousness is available because I go to the Father, and you will see me no more.

  11 Judgment will come because the ruler of this world has already been judged.

  12 There is so much more I want to tell you, but you can't bear it now.

  13 **When the Spirit of truth comes, he will guide you into all truth.** He will not speak on his own but will tell you what he has heard. **He will tell you about the future.**

  14 He will **bring me glory** by telling you whatever he receives from me.

  15 All that belongs to the Father is mine; this is why I said, 'The Spirit will tell you whatever he receives from me.'

- Acts 1:8 NLT (Jesus): But **you will receive power when the Holy Spirit comes upon you**. And you will be my witnesses, telling people about me everywhere—in Jerusalem, throughout Judea, in Samaria, and to the ends of the earth.

The Holy Spirit Fills Us With Power to Miracles

It is the mighty Holy Spirit who fills us with the power to do signs, wonders, and miracles:

- Acts 10:38 NIV:
  God anointed Jesus of Nazareth **with the Holy Spirit and with power. Then** Jesus went around doing good and healing all who were oppressed by the devil, **for God was with him.**

- Luke 4:17-19 NIV:
  17 and the scroll of the prophet Isaiah was handed to (Jesus). Unrolling it, he found the place where it is written:
  18 '**The Spirit of the Lord is on me, because he has anointed me** to proclaim good news to the poor. **He has sent me** to proclaim freedom for the prisoners **and recovery of sight for the blind, to set the oppressed free,**
  19 to proclaim the year of the Lord's favor.'

- Acts 6:8,10 NLT:
  6 Stephen, a man full of God's grace and power, **performed amazing miracles and signs among the people.** [...]
  10 None of [Stephen's enemies] could stand against **the wisdom and the Spirit** with which Stephen spoke.

Here is a reminder to us to constantly pursue and stay close to the source of our power:

- Luke 5:15-17 NLT:
  15 But despite Jesus' instructions, the report of **his power** spread even faster, and vast crowds came to hear him preach and to be healed of their diseases.
  16 **But Jesus often withdrew to the wilderness for prayer.**

Receiving the Holy Spirit vs. the New Birth

Given From the following scripture passage, it can be clearly seen that the new birth in Jesus Christ is a separate experience from receiving the Holy Spirit in His fullness:

- Acts 8:14-17 NLT:

14 When the apostles in Jerusalem heard that the people of Samaria had accepted God's message, they sent Peter and John there.

15 As soon as they arrived, they prayed for these new believers to receive the Holy Spirit.

16 The Holy Spirit had not yet come upon any of them, for they had only been baptized in the name of the Lord Jesus.

17 Then Peter and John laid their hands upon these believers, **and they received the Holy Spirit.**

If you have not yet experienced your own personal Pentecost (Acts chapter 2), we urge you to make this a priority. Ask your Pastor or another Spirit-filled believer to pray with you to receive the infilling of the Holy Spirit or stay after this class so we can pray for you.

It is the mighty Holy Spirit who fills us with the power to do signs, wonders, and miracles:

- Acts 10:38 NIV:

God anointed Jesus of Nazareth **with the Holy Spirit and with power. Then** Jesus went around doing good and healing all who were oppressed by the devil, **for God was with him.**

- Luke 4:17-19 NIV:

17 and the scroll of the prophet Isaiah was handed to (Jesus). Unrolling it, he found the place where it is written:

18 **'The Spirit of the Lord is on me, because he has anointed me** to proclaim good news to the poor. **He has sent me** to proclaim freedom for the prisoners **and recovery of sight for the blind, to set the oppressed free,**

19 to proclaim the year of the Lord's favor.'

- Acts 6:8,10 NLT:

6 Stephen, a man full of God's grace and power, **performed amazing miracles and signs among the people.** [...]

10 None of [Stephen's enemies] could stand against **the wisdom and the Spirit** with which Stephen spoke.

Here is a reminder to us to constantly pursue and stay close to the source of our power:

- Luke 5:15-17 NLT:

  15 But despite Jesus' instructions, the report of **his power** spread even faster, and vast crowds came to hear him preach and to be healed of their diseases.
  16 **But Jesus often withdrew to the wilderness for prayer.**

Receiving the Holy Spirit vs. the New Birth

Given the following scripture passage, it can be clearly seen that the new birth in Jesus Christ is a separate experience from receiving the Holy Spirit in His fullness:

- Acts 8:14-17 NLT:

  14 When the apostles in Jerusalem heard that the people of Samaria had accepted God's message, they sent Peter and John there.
  15 As soon as they arrived, they prayed for these new believers to receive the Holy Spirit.
  16 **The Holy Spirit had not yet come upon any of them, for they had only been baptized in the name of the Lord Jesus.**
  17 Then Peter and John laid their hands upon these believers, **and they received the Holy Spirit.**

If you have not yet experienced your own personal Pentecost (see Acts chapter 2), make this a priority. Ask your Pastor or another Spirit-filled believer to pray with you to receive the infilling of the Holy Spirit or stay after this class so we can pray for you (if this is one of our in-person classes).

12

Appendix B: Recommended Material

THIS SECTION CONTAINS A LIST of books and videos which are complementary to the mission and purpose of our *Extreme Faith for Extreme Evangelism* class.

12.1 Recommended Books

- *Expect to Believe: 90 Bible Devotionals to Increase Your Faith For the Impossible*, by Paul Williams, Life of Faith in Christ Ministries.

- *Breaking Generational Curses & Ungodly Vows*, by Life of Faith in Christ Ministries.

- *The Believer's Authority*, by Kenneth E. Hagin.

- *School of the Spirit: Developing the Human Spirit*, by Roberts Liardon

- *The Seer Expanded Edition: The Prophetic Power of Visions, Dreams and Open Heavens*, by James W. Goll.

- *Seeing the Supernatural: How to Sense, Discern and Battle in the Spiritual Realm*, by Jennifer Eivaz

- *The Modern Seer: A biblical gift in today's context*, by Jim Driscoll.

- *Accessing the Courts of Heaven: Positioning Yourself for Breakthrough and Answered Prayers*, by Robert Henderson.

- *Operating in the Courts of Heaven: Granting God the Legal Rights to Fulfill His Passion and Answer Our Prayers*, by Robert Henderson.

- *Prayers and Declarations that Open the Courts of Heaven (The Official Courts of Heaven Book 4)*, by Robert Henderson.

- *Interpreting Dreams (plus updated & revised Dream Dictionary)*, by Ed Traut.

12.2 Recommended Videos

- *"How to Keep the Fire of the Holy Spirit Burning - 3 Keys"* by David Diga Hernandez:
  https://youtu.be/tDPbNz4phUQ
  (28 minutes)

- Here is a spectacular case history example our absolute power over evil spirits and evil men who are controlled by evil spirits:

  o *"I Was Shot Repeatedly But a Force Stopped the Bullets! | Terry Mize"*
    Sid Roth It's Supernatural:
    https://youtu.be/_NS9a_ie4Co

- We recommend that you watch all three videos in the order listed here, and a single continuous viewing session, if at all possible, in order to receive a balanced view of the presented material:

  o *John Ramirez Revealing Satan's tactics:*
    https://youtu.be/LkeJad8UeSE
    (14 minutes 27 seconds)

  o *Ex-Satan Worshipper John Ramirez Testimony:*
    https://youtu.be/I11L71PD3Lw
    (37 minutes 11 seconds)

  o *Unmasking Satan | John Ramirez | Sid Roth's It's Supernatural:*
    https://youtu.be/_ZK0Z8Mz-Rs
    (28 minutes 31 seconds)

Made in the USA
Monee, IL
12 May 2025

17344194R00142